Beadpoint

Beautiful Bead Stitching on Canvas

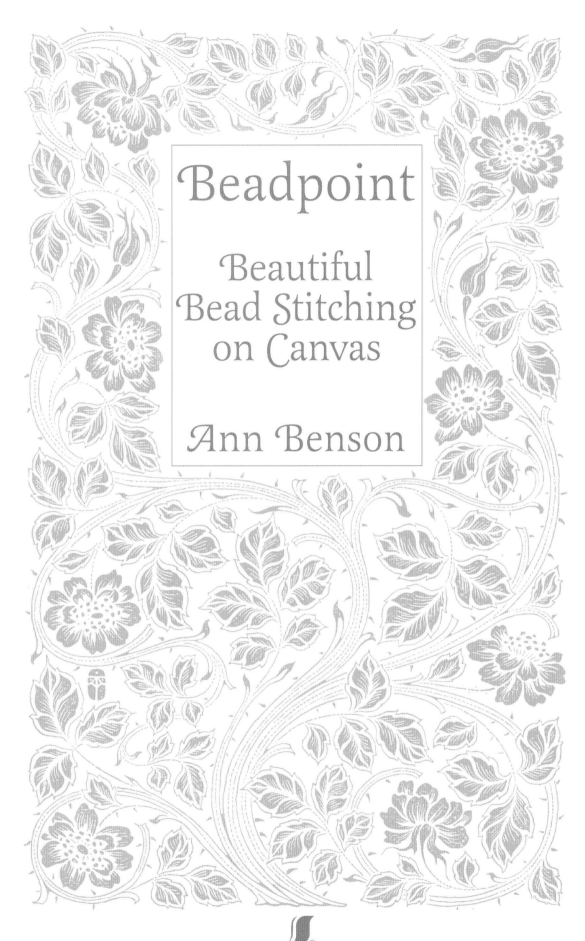

Beadpoint

Beautiful Bead Stitching on Canvas

Ann Benson

Sterling Publishing Co., Inc. New York
A Sterling/Chapelle Book

Chapelle Ltd.

- Owner: Jo Packham
- Editor: Leslie Farmer
- Photography: Kevin Dilley for Hazen Photography
- Photo Stylist: Jill Dahlberg
- Staff: Areta Bingham, Kass Burchett, Ray Cornia, Marilyn Goff, Karla Haberstich,
  Holly Hollingsworth, Susan Jorgensen, Barbara Milburn, Karmen Quinney, Caroll Shreeve,
  Cindy Stoeckl, Kim Taylor, Sara Toliver, Desirée Wybrow

If you have any questions or comments, please contact:
Chapelle, Ltd., Inc., P.O. Box 9252, Ogden, UT 84409
(801) 621-2777 • (801) 621-2788 Fax
e-mail: chapelle@chapelleltd.com   web site: chapelleltd.com

Library of Congress Cataloging-in-Publication Data

Benson, Ann.
    Beadpoint : beautiful bead stitching on canvas / Ann Benson.
        p. cm.
    Includes index.
    ISBN 0-8069-8939-4
        1. Canvas embroidery--Patterns. 2. Beadwork--Patterns. I. Title:
Beautiful bead stitching on canvas. II. Title.

TT778.C3 B445 2002
746.5--dc21

2002030674

10 9 8 7 6 5 4 3 2 1

Published by Sterling Publishing Co., Inc.
387 Park Avenue South, New York, NY 10016
©2003 by Ann Benson
Distributed in Canada by Sterling Publishing
c/o Canadian Manda Group, One Atlantic Avenue, Suite 105
Toronto, Ontario, Canada M6K 3E7
Distributed in Great Britain by Chrysalis Books
64 Brewery Road, London N7 9NT, England
Distributed in Australia by Capricorn Link (Australia) Pty. Ltd.
P.O. Box 704, Windsor, NSW 2756, Australia
Printed in China
All Rights Reserved

Sterling ISBN 0-8069-8939-4

Thanks

We would like to thank the following friends and businesses who so graciously allowed us to use their personal and professional spaces as settings for the photographs in this book: Ned and Margaret Favero; and Ruby & Begonia of Ogden, Utah.

Write Us

If you have any questions regarding supplies and/or materials, please contact the author via e-mail: comments@annbenson.com

Table of Contents

Beadpoint

Beadpoint is a very elegant needlework technique that was widely popular at the height of Victorian times.

The most commonly available type of bead, the seed bead, takes the shape of a flattened sphere, or, if you prefer, dimensional oval—the same shape as a traditional needlepoint stitch made with wool or other fibers. In beadpoint, beads are sewn onto canvas diagonally and at the same left-to-right slant as a regular needlepoint stitch.

The finished look of beadpoint and needlepoint are very similar—the main difference is in the texture. Many beads have lustered or metallic finishes and, therefore, reflect light, whereas traditional needlepoint fibers—wool, cotton, linen—do not. Rather, they tend to absorb light, so the resulting look is quite soft. Beads open up a whole new world of texture and color to the needlepointer.

Beads can be used in combination with fibers to create a multimedia look. An example of this is the Floral Pillow on page 44.

Because needlepoint canvas is substantial and holds it shape, beadpoint is an especially good technique for use in wearables such as handbags and belts.

Any size piece of beadpoint can be worked, with the only limit being the weight—glass is extremely heavy.

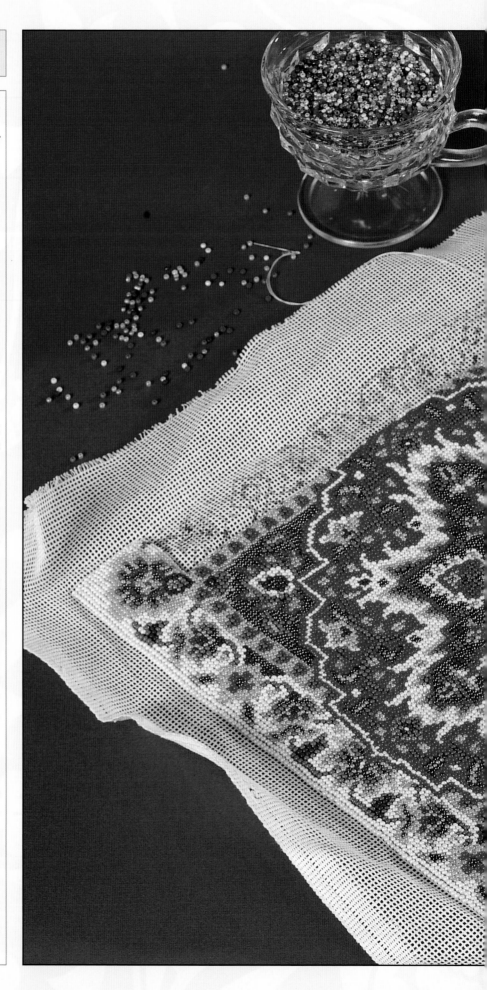

About the Beads Used in Beadpoint

The designs in this book use seed beads almost exclusively. Other types of beads, such as bugle beads, pearls, and fancy glass beads, are added only as embellishments and do not constitute the body of the design.

Bead Sizes

There are several sizes of seed beads that can be used for beadpoint, all of which are roughly similar to a single stitch in traditional needlepoint.

Size 11/0 seed beads are the most common size and are available in a wide range of colors and finishes. Size 11/0 seed beads are manufactured in Japan, the Czech Republic, Taiwan, and India. In this book, we use Japanese and Czech beads because of their reliability of availability. Czech beads are often sold in hanks, and tend to have more variation in shape. They tend to be flatter and have smaller holes than most Japanese beads. If you want perfect uniformity in your beads, you may want to avoid Czech beads, but we have used them liberally throughout this book because there is a certain natural loveliness to them that is the result of their slight irregularities.

These photos illustrate the color palette available in 15/0 seed beads. This size bead is manufactured in both Japan and the Czech Republic. The designs shown in this book use Japanese 15/0 seed beads exclusively as they are easier to use than their Czech counterparts. The Japanese beads have a good range of colors and large holes relative to the tiny size of the beads.

(Right) 15/0 seed beads in red and orange tones. (Below) 15/0 seed beads in green and aqua tones. (Opposite Top) 15/0 seed beads in rose and orchid tones. (Opposite Bottom) 15/0 seed beads in blue and purple tones.

Size 11/0 seed beads can be used with needlepoint canvas that has 14 stitches to the inch, usually referred to as #14 inter-lock canvas.

Size 15/0 seed beads (shown right, on opposite page, and on page 14) are manufactured in Japan and the Czech Republic. Japanese 15/0 seed beads are the only type used in this book. Czech 15/0 seed beads are not recommended because the holes are often too small to fit over even the smallest beading nee-dle. They can be quite frustrat-ing. Japanese seed beads have a good range of colors, and most have surprisingly large holes rela-tive to the tiny size of the bead.

They are best used on #18 interlock canvas; you can get astonishing detail in design using 15/0 seed beads.

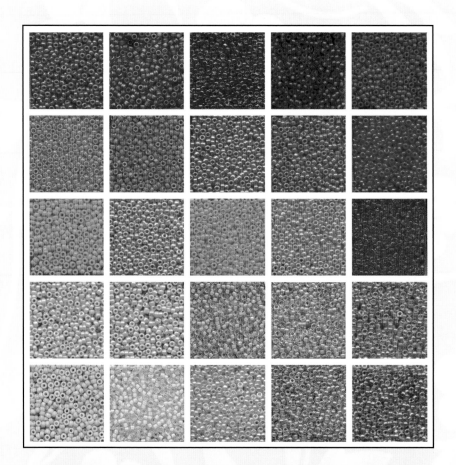

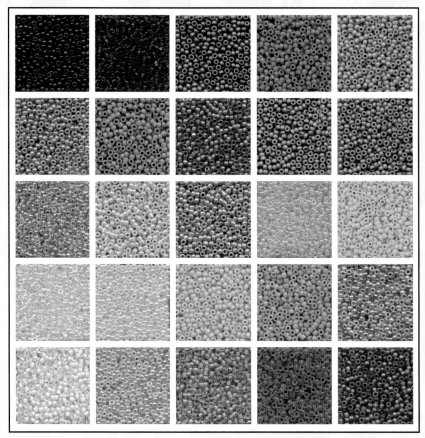

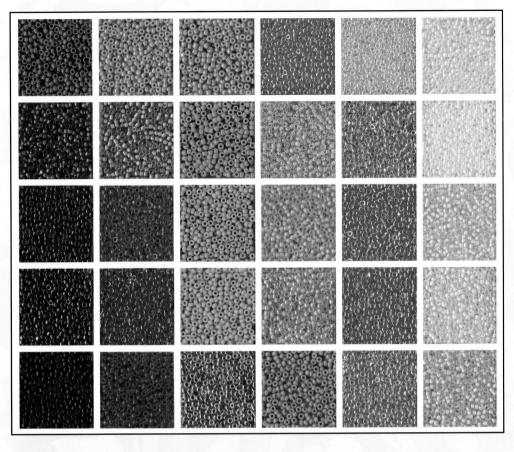

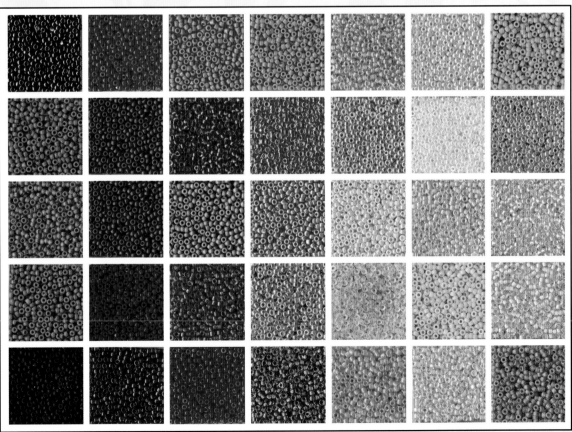

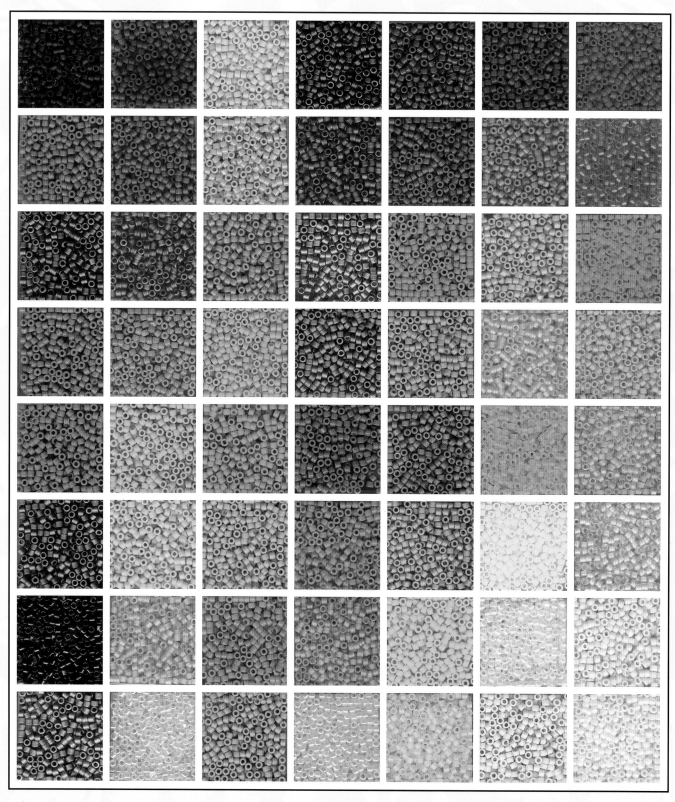

(Above) Slightly tubular Delica beads are shown from black and gray to blue-green to green to yellow and tan to orange and peach tones.

Though they are called seed beads because of their general shape, Delica beads (shown above and on opposite page) are in a class by themselves.

Delicas are made exclusively in Japan. They are slightly tubular in shape, have very thin walls and, therefore, good sized holes. There is an astounding assortment of colors and finishes available in Delicas, and they are a joy to use.

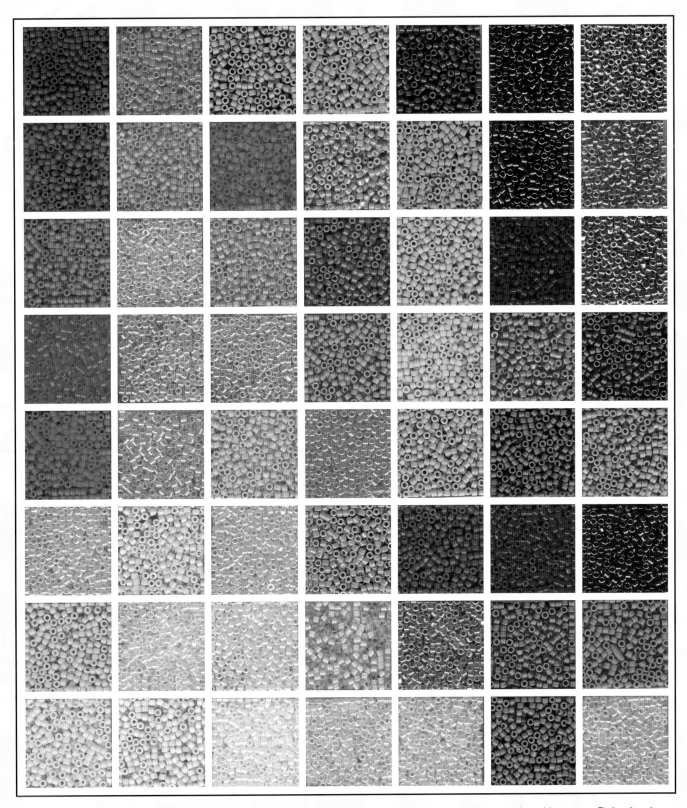

(Above) More colors in the Delica bead palette—from red to pink and rose to orchid and lavender to purple to blue tones. Delica beads are best used on #16 duo canvas.

Delica beads do tend to be a bit more expensive than 11/0 and 15/0 seed beads for the same coverage area. However, since most of the pieces in this book are relatively small, they are not necessarily prohibitive.

Delicas may only be used on #16 interlock canvas, and are best used on the duo variety, which will be described in the section on canvas.

13

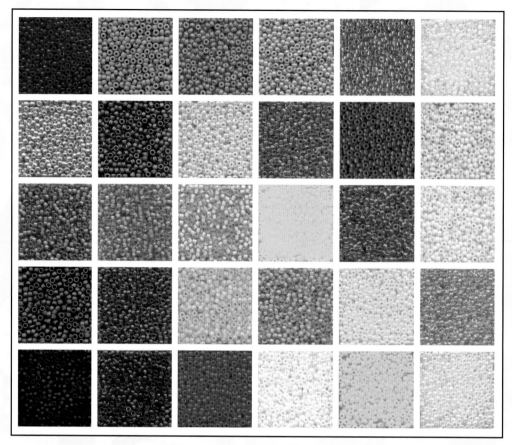

(Right) This photo shows 15/0 seed beads in brown and yellow tones. Though this is a limited palette, there are several different bead types represented such as, solid-colored beads in the opaque, matte opaque, lined, galvanized, Ceylon, and opaque lustered varieties and matte transparent beads which do not look transparent.

Bead Colors

The glass used to create seed beads is colored with chemicals and molten metals. Because the coloring agents become part of the glass itself, most beads are extremely colorfast and will wash well. There are two major exceptions to this rule, notably dyed beads, where the color is "fused" to the outer surface of the bead, and galvanized beads, where the metallic finish is applied to the glass surface. Dyed and galvanized beads should not be used in anything that will require regular washing.

Beads with colors that appear solid are the best choice for use in beadpoint. There are several different types of solid-colored beads, such as opaque, matte opaque, lined, galvanized, Ceylon, opaque lustered, and matte transparent which do not look transparent.

Transparent beads are not suitable for beadpoint for two reasons: 1) the thread is visible inside them; and 2) the white of the canvas will show through.

In traditional needlepoint, you can use several different shades of one color in a design, perhaps as many as seven, depending on the subtlety of the wool dyer's range on the color card. Not so in beads—if you get five shades of one color, you are lucky!

Because of the limited chemical process used to create the bead colors, there are only so many variations available. In certain shades, such as the yellow family and the olive greens, the limitations are more severe. However, with a little creativity, a limited color palette may span further than you might expect.

Figuring the Needed Amounts of Each Color

Seed beads and Delica beads are sold by metric weights, i.e., grams and portions of kilograms. Packet sizes vary from one vendor to the next—one company may sell a 7.5 gram tube of a particular color, while another company sells a 10 gram plastic bag of the same color. More expensive beads, such as those with 24-karat gold finish, may be sold in amounts as small as 3 grams per pack. Use the numbers indicated in the materials list for each project and the guidelines below to figure the amounts you will need to purchase.

Size 11/0 seed beads can be purchased in tubes, plastic bag packs, and hanks (Czech beads). Japanese beads are not sold in hanks.

1 gram = 100 beads
1 teaspoon = 5 grams = 500 beads
12 hanks = approximately .5 kilogram
1 hank = approximately 4000 beads

Size 15/0 seed beads are generally sold in 20–40 gram packages at retail. They can also be purchased in larger amounts, usually 100 grams or 250 grams.

1 gram = 220 beads
1 teaspoon = 5 grams = 1100 beads

Delica beads can be purchased in tubes and plastic bag packs.

1 gram = 200 beads
1 teaspoon = 5 grams = 1000 beads

These are rough equivalents; there can be some variance in the number of beads per gram, depending on the finish and color of the bead.

In general, beads with metallic finishes (iris, galvanized) are heavier than unfinished beads, thus there are fewer beads per gram. Beads with matte finishes have had some of their surface taken off in processing and are minutely lighter, so there are more beads per gram.

Another consideration is the inevitable presence of "blem" beads, those that are misshapen or broken, and therefore unusable. A safe rule of thumb is to buy 15% more than you think you will need.

Organizing Materials

Having materials well organized almost guarantees the smooth progress of beadwork. I recommend keeping one or two grams of each color bead in a small separate box. Draw from these boxes to replenish colors in a mix that is kept in another larger box.

You should also have on hand craft, embroidery, and fabric scissors, an assortment of beading and sewing needles, dressmaker's pins, thread, findings, etc. Keep them all together in a box or tray that is easily accessible.

(Above) A practical way of organizing your materials is found in using small acrylic boxes to hold beads of a color and size. Place these boxes in a larger utility box within reach together with beading and sewing needles, findings, scissors, etc.

Interlock Canvas

Interlock canvas has thicker threads than duo canvas, and is stiffer when handled. The holes are good sized and easy to see. Passing the needle through the holes is very easy. The intersections of the woven threads are extremely stable and will not shift unless you apply considerable pressure.

Size #18 interlock canvas is perfect for use with 15/0 seed beads. These are the smallest beads for which there is a substantial color selection; they are also probably the smallest beads that can practicably be used, as smaller beads tend to have smaller holes, and will become stuck on the needle. Either superhuman eyesight or constant magnification would be needed to work with anything smaller.

Painting your design onto #18 canvas presents no particular challenge. This canvas is wonderfully adaptable to computer printing.

(Right) Here is a small sample of #18 interlock canvas. Due to the small size of the weave, it is best used with 15/0 seed beads.

Size #14 interlock canvas is probably the most widely used canvas for traditional needlepoint. Prepainted canvases are easy to find in this size in fine needlework stores. Size 11/0 seed beads, both Czech and Japanese, can be easily used on #14 interlock canvas.

Because it is thicker than #18 interlock canvas, #14 interlock canvas does not work as well on computer printers, but it may work if your printer has a setting for card stock.

Design possibilities with #14 interlock canvas are unlimited because the selection of colors in 11/0 seed beads is phenomenal. Additionally, it

is very easy to combine threadwork and beadwork in one design on this size canvas.

(Right) A sample of #14 interlock canvas shows that the weave is comparably larger than #18 interlock canvas. Size 11/0 seed beads are best used with #14 interlock canvas.

Duo Canvas

Duo literally means "double," which is the defining characteristic of this canvas. The threads are finer than those used in interlock or mono canvas and are closely paired in the weave.

The weave is relatively stable, but the feel of the fabric is very supple. For this reason, duo canvas is particularly good for use in clothing items. Simply put, it lays well.

Duo canvas is available in many different sizes. However, the best beadpoint effect is yielded when matching #16 duo canvas with Delica beads.

It may take a few rows on the first duo canvas project to become accustomed to the small opening through which the needle passes, but once you get the hang of it, the work will proceed as smoothly as working on interlock.

Another advantage of working with duo canvas is that it is easy to paint a design on it. Because there is more thread surface to accept color, applying the color is a breeze.

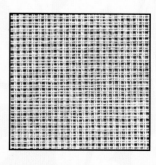

(Right) Duo canvas is woven of fine paired threads. Although many different sizes are available in duo canvas, the best effect is yielded when matching #16 duo canvas, as shown, with Delica beads.

Working from a Chart

Designs are often worked from charted patterns. The patterns in this book are specifically designed for use with beads and were created with the seed bead palette in mind.

Cross-stitch embroidery charts are often used for beadpoint, but care must be taken to select patterns that have no more than three or, at most, four shades of any one color to avoid difficulty matching bead colors to suggested embroidery colors.

You may wish to make a color photocopy of the charts in this book and, when counting a design, mark off each row as it is completed to help keep your place. Work in rows to avoid confusion; skipping around from row to row is not recommended. When using a chart that does not show beads as part of the color bar, we recommend taping or sewing a few beads of the chosen color next to the appropriate color key on the color bar, so the bead that goes with each symbol can be easily identified.

Using Blank Charts

The blank charts on pages 120–126 are intended to make it possible for you to do your own designing.

Copies of charts can be enlarged as desired for ease in designing. This will not affect stitch count.

The shaped charts are intended for use with the size of canvas called for on the modeled project. For example, the blank scissors case chart should only be worked on #18 canvas, using 15/0 seed beads, or it will be oversized. Likewise, the blank jeweled purse chart is designed to fit the standard 2½" purse handle, so it should also be stitched, using 15/0 seed beads on #18 canvas.

(Above) If possible, make a color photocopy of the desired design chart and, when counting the design, mark off each row as it is completed to help keep your place.

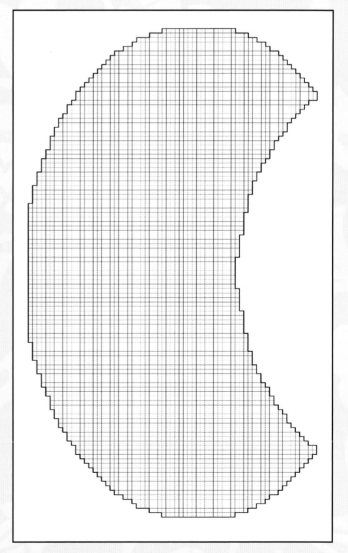

(Above) Blank charts like this one, which has been reduced to 75%, are included on pages 120–126 in the case that you should wish to do your own designing.

Adding Odd-shaped Beads to Your Own Designs

If you want to add texture and interest to your designs, you may want to include some fancy beads. In this book, there are a few designs that use larger seed beads and bugle beads. These are relatively predictable in shape and size and can reliably be used.

However, if you want to add other shapes such as semiprecious chips and pearls, you can certainly do that. Place the odd-shaped beads on the design grid and outline them, then work your design around the outlines.

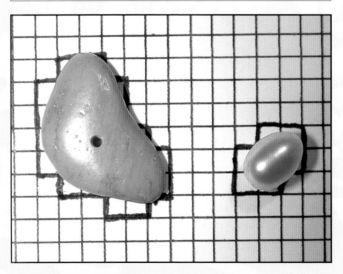

(Above) When charting your own design, place the odd-shaped bead on a chart sized the same as the canvas you intend to use. Outline the bead to the square, then work your design around the outlines.

Putting the Design on the Canvas

The charts included in this book are designed to make it easy for you to read the pattern as you stitch from row to row. However, we have always found that the beading is more enjoyable and progresses more quickly if the design is first applied to the canvas in color.

In traditional needlepoint, the design is almost always printed or painted directly onto the canvas, and rarely charted. The two most common commercial methods used for this process are screen printing, where each color is applied separately; and heat-transfer printing, where the entire design is printed in reverse onto a piece of paper, using sublimation dyes, and then transferred onto the canvas by heat sublimation. There are several good methods you can use at home to apply your design directly to the canvas.

Fine quality canvases are created by a method known as stitch painting, where each stitch is painted in its proper color on the canvas. The painting is done from a charted design and the colors are accurate.

With this type of painted canvas, you will not have to make design decisions as you stitch, since they will have been made before applying the color. Acrylic paints and oils paints are most often used for this type of canvas.

Additionally, an outline can be drawn on the canvas, then stitched using the outline as a guide. In this case you will need to make design decisions as you stitch, which can be frustrating if the decision about which color to use in which position turns out to be less effective than desired.

In a similar fashion, a rough color representation of the design can be painted directly onto the canvas. There will be fewer decisions to make when using this method. Permanent color fabric markers, sold in most commercial fabric and craft stores, are excellent for use in applying color to canvas. The color selection is limited, however, and it can be an expensive undertaking, depending on the number of colors being used in the design.

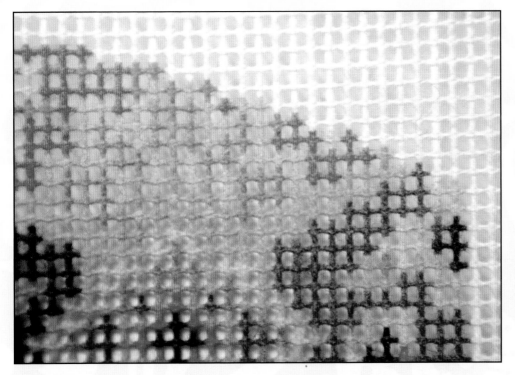

(Left) For ease in stitching, first apply the colors of the design directly onto your canvas. This can be accomplished by using permanent colored fabric markers or by working up the design on a computer and printing it onto the canvas. Size #18 interlock canvas runs through the manual feed of a printer quite easily. Size #14 interlock canvas may be used if your printer has a setting for card stock.

A favorite method of applying color to a canvas is to work up the design on a computer and print the color directly from the computer printer onto the canvas. By experimenting with sizing of the computer file, the stitches will usually fall into place.

Adobe®'s Photoshop® software was used to develop and print these designs. There are many excellent needlework graphing programs that enable you to size your design (most importantly, in stitches per inch) so the stitches will land well when printed.

Print the design on paper first, then tape the canvas to that piece of paper to position it properly for printing. Set the printer in the card stock position, then print again.

The one disadvantage of this method is that the color in most computer printers is not permanent and will bleed if the piece is wet-blocked. The solution to that problem is to bleach out the color prior to blocking. Be certain to test your beads for colorfastness in a similar solution of bleach prior to immersing the entire piece.

Preparing the Canvas Prior to Stitching

The stitching will go more smoothly if you prepare the canvas in certain ways before beginning the work. First, it is important to determine the actual size needed for a project. Since canvas can vary slightly in count from one piece to the next, it is important to determine the actual count.

This can be done by measuring a 4" section, counting the threads, and then dividing by four. This should be done in both directions of the weave.

You may find that the weave in one direction is actually 13.9 stitches to the inch, and 14.1 in the other. Manufacturers of canvas do their best to ensure the weave is as consistent as possible, but some variation should be expected.

Once you have determined the canvas count, determine the finished measurement of the design by dividing that into the number of squares in the chart. The designs in this book include the stitch counts in both directions. Add 1" to each side all around, unless the design is very small, in which case ¾" is probably adequate. A larger margin may feel cumbersome while stitching.

After determining the size required, cut the canvas carefully along the weave. Tape the canvas all around with masking tape as shown below and round the edges slightly. This will prevent the beading thread from tangling in the rough edge of the canvas, and will eliminate the problem of threads raveling as the canvas is handled.

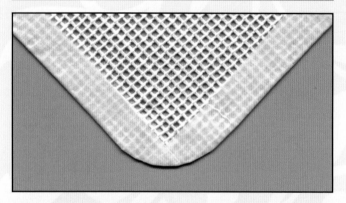

(Above) Before stitching, take time to prepare the canvas by taping all around the edges with masking tape. This will prevent the canvas threads from raveling.

If the canvas becomes softer as you stitch, it may be necessary to apply ordinary laundry spray starch to it. The stiffness in canvas comes from a finishing agent applied during the manufacturing process; it is water soluble in most cases, so wetting the canvas will loosen it. There may be some occasions when this is desirable, such as in clothing uses. But in general, it is a good idea to maintain the canvas stiffness.

Thread

The thread has one purpose—to hold the bead on the canvas. It is not necessary to use a thread that is specifically designed for use with beads. While some of those threads have some advantages, for example, resistance to fraying from sharp-edged beads, there is little to be gained in their use.

Ordinary mercerized cotton or cotton-wrapped polyester sewing thread—there are racks and racks of it in every fabric store in almost any desired color—is quite acceptable.

A light gray or white is recommended for stitching most projects since the thread barely shows. Otherwise, match the color to the general overall tone of your project; if the bead colors are on the dark side, use a darker neutral color.

(Right) White or light gray thread can be used for stitching most projects. Although the beads being stitched in this illustration are deep red, it is not necessary to use the same color thread.

Conditioning the Thread

Your stitching will progress more smoothly if the thread is conditioned before using it. Cut a length of thread, then run it over a cake of beeswax or solid hand soap. This will minimize tangling. Additionally, there are good commercial thread conditioners available from most beading supply catalogs.

Threading the Needle

In comparison to needles used for traditional needlepoint, the eyes on needles used for beading are very small.

Cut the end of the thread clean with sharp scissors before attempting to insert the thread through the needle eye.

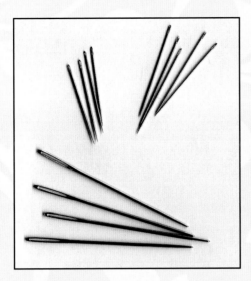

(Right) Note the striking difference between #11 "between" needles (top), used for beadpoint, and #20 tapestry needles (bottom), used for traditional needlepoint.

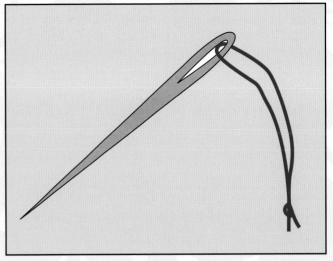

(Above) In this illustration, the thread is doubled on the needle and "closed" or looped through the eye of the needle. Closed-end threading is recommended to avoid having the thread slip out of the eye of the needle.

Double the thread on the needle. It can be either open or closed, depending on your preference. However, closed-end threading is recommended because the thread cannot slip out of the eye of the needle as it can in open-end threading.

The work can be streamlined if you thread several needles at one time—I often have as many as six threaded needles lined up and waiting.

To make working with multiple needles easier, cut a piece of white flannel into which you can insert threaded needles into when not in use.

Attaching the Thread to the Canvas

The first thread on any piece is always the most difficult to attach, since there are no back-threads in which to secure it.

Use your fingertip to hold a length of thread on the back of the canvas. Stitch over the thread for several stitches until it is secure. Thereafter, you should attach each new thread within the back-threads, then bring it to the surface to continue stitching.

You may use knots, but they should be very small so as not to raise the surface of the bead-point if the item is framed or applied to another surface. It is better to avoid knots if possible.

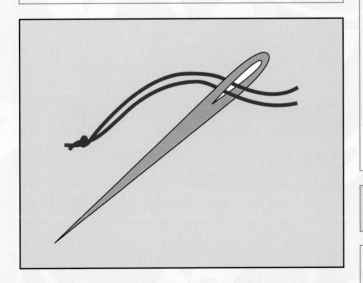

(Above) In this illustration, the thread is doubled on the needle and "open" or easily removed from the eye of the needle. Thread several needles at once to streamline your work.

Stitching Technique

There are many similarities between bead-point and traditional needlepoint. Both create images that consist of patterned dots of color. Both slant from left at bottom to right at top.

Two of needlepoint's standard stitches, the continental and half-cross, are used in beadpoint. The long backstitch method of beadpoint is similar to the continental stitch. The short backstitch method corresponds to half-cross stitch. Note the path of the thread as each bead is attached to the canvas.

Short Backstitch/Half-cross Stitch

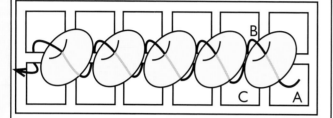

Long Backstitch/Continental Stitch

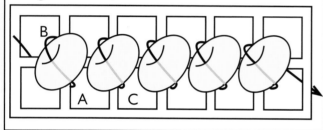

Work the design in alternating horizontal rows of long and short backstitches. This "combination" method results in a beaded piece with good "weight" but very little canvas distortion.

(Above) The long backstitch moves from left to right along the horizontal row. This stitch should be combined with the short backstitch on the return trip across the canvas.

If the short backstitch method is used alone, the threading on the back of the canvas is very minimal, making it difficult to anchor new threads and tie off finished ones. If only the long backstitch method is used, the back of the canvas becomes heavily padded with thread, causing significant distortion of the finished piece.

Again, using a combination of the two stitching methods ensures a good backing with minimal distortion. It is important to take distortion into consideration when stitching since, when distortion does occur, the beadpoint piece must be reshaped with blocking in a manner similar to that used for regular needlepoint.

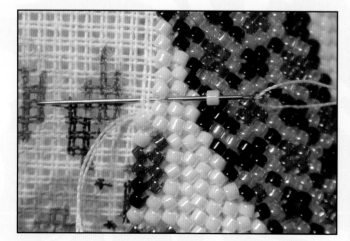

(Above) Beads are worked in horizontal rows, from right to left, using the short backstitch. This stitch is similar to the half-cross stitch used in traditional needlepoint. In beadpoint, the short backstitch is most effective when alternating it with the long backstitch.

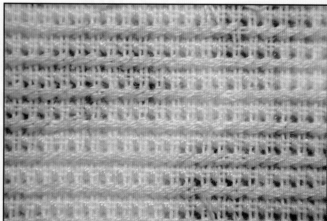

(Above) Observe the completed stitching from the back of the piece. The design is worked in alternating horizontal rows of long and short backstitches. This method results in a beaded piece with good "weight" but very little canvas distortion.

Combining Beads & Fibers

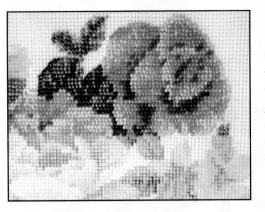

When stitching a design in which the background is fiber (such as the Floral Pillow on page 44), stitch the beaded foreground first. If there are decisions to be made on a printed canvas, make them in favor of the beaded area, not the background, as the beaded area is the visual basis for the design.

Begin the beading at the top segment of a design area and work downward by horizontal rows. As you progress, the segments will meet up, and eventually you will have continuous rows along the width of design. Similarly, as you come to the bottom of the piece, you will separate off into smaller beading areas, which will later be surrounded by fiber stitches.

(Left and Below) For a design that combines beads and fibers, stitch the beaded foreground first, then fill in around the beaded area with wool. Stitch the beading from top to bottom in horizontal rows as indicated on the charted design.

23

Finishing a Thread

You should end your thread when there is still at least 3" of length left. If you allow the thread to become shorter than that, you will find it difficult to pick up a bead—you literally have to drag the canvas with you. Better to waste a few inches of thread than to disturb your "pile" of beads.

To secure the thread, run it under a few long backthreads on the back of the canvas, then clip it close, taking care not to clip any stitching threads.

Try to avoid finishing a thread in the same backthreads as those in which a thread has been attached, or the thread buildup will be too thick, and an uneven front surface may result.

Reshaping the Beaded Canvas Before Finishing

If you have used the alternate row method of stitching the beads onto the canvas, you are not likely to have severe distortion in your beadwork. If you do, however, there are some guidelines that you should follow in restoring the beadwork to its proper shape.

The simpler method, which works quite well with smaller pieces, is to steam the threads on the back of the canvas and stretch the piece back to shape while the threads are still warm. Because the sizing on canvas is water soluble, it will "loosen" during the steaming process. As the canvas and threads cool, the sizing will reset in the new shape. This should always be done before any excess canvas is trimmed away from the beadwork, as you will need some gripping room to stretch it.

Place the beadwork face-down on a clean white cloth on your ironing board. Set the iron at a high temperature with full steam. If your iron has a "burst of steam" feature, use that. Saturate the threads with steam and reshape the piece before it cools. Hold it in position until the back threads are cool. Be very careful not to touch the beads themselves until you are sure they are completely cooled—remember, glass holds heat for a long time.

The second method, used frequently in regular needlepoint, is the wet-block method. Leave the tape around the edges of the canvas, then immerse it in water.

If you have applied nonpermanent color to the canvas prior to stitching, the color will probably bleed. This will not have any adverse effect on the beads; you do not need to be concerned about it unless the beadpoint is to be used as part of a garment. In that case, I recommend soaking the piece in a weak solution of bleach prior to wet-blocking. This should remove all unwanted color from the canvas. Bleach will not remove acrylic or oil paint, permanent markers, or heat-transferred designs, but these are not likely to run in the first place.

The piece should be thoroughly rinsed before blocking. Pat out the excess water with paper towels or a clean towel—do not ring or squeeze the piece under any circumstances.

Straighten the canvas by gently stretching it, then position it on a clean, unfinished wood board. Using staples or rustproof tacks, secure the stretched beadwork to a board. Allow it to dry thoroughly before removing the staples or tacks, using needlenosed pliers if necessary.

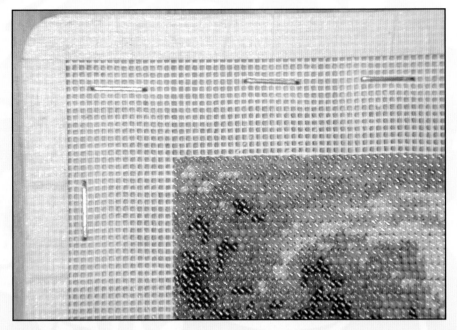

(Left) Reshape a distorted canvas using the wet-block method. Leaving the tape around the edges of the canvas, immerse the finished beadwork in water. Remove the piece from the water and pat out excess with a paper towel. Gently stretch the canvas and place it on a clean piece of unfinished wood. Secure the canvas to the board with staples or tacks. Allow the canvas to dry, then remove the staples or tacks.

(Below) Reshaping or blocking a distorted canvas is especially important when the beaded piece is set into a frame.

Apple Button Cover

This design must be stitched on #18 interlock canvas, using 15/0 seed beads. The finished beadwork will be mounted on a standard 1½" purchased coverable-button form.

Stitch count: 29 x 29

Materials required:
Beads:
  15/0 seed beads:
    Ceylon light green (10)
    Ceylon light pink (26)
    lined medium pink (59)
    opaque brick red (27)
    opaque dark green (13)
    opaque medium green (26)
    opaque red (204)
    opaque yellow (300)

Misc:
  Coverable-button form, 1½"
  #18 interlock canvas, 3" square
  Needles
  Scissors

Instructions:
1. Stitch as charted on opposite page.

Finishing:
1. Trim excess canvas to ⅜". Notch all around to accommodate bending.

2. Following manufacturer's instructions, cover button form with finished beadwork.

Bead Code

opaque yellow

Ceylon light green

opaque medium green

opaque dark green

Ceylon light pink

lined medium pink

opaque red

opaque brick red

Apple Button Cover Chart

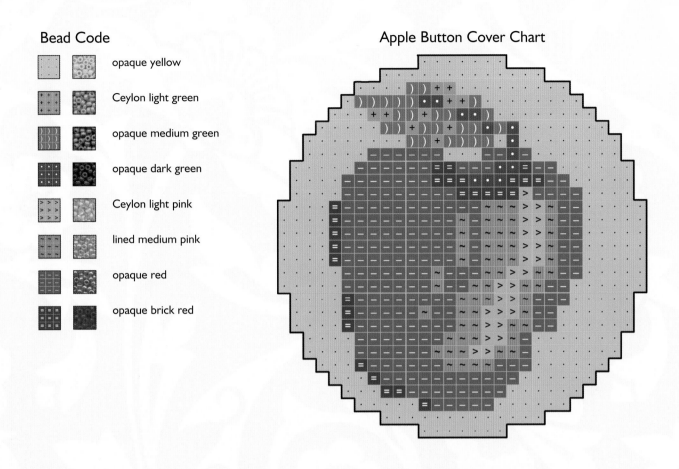

Bead Code

lustered ivory (280)

Ceylon light blue (152)

Ceylon medium periwinkle (104)

lustered medium blue (72)

lined orchid (48)

matte red AB (9)

Alternate Design Chart

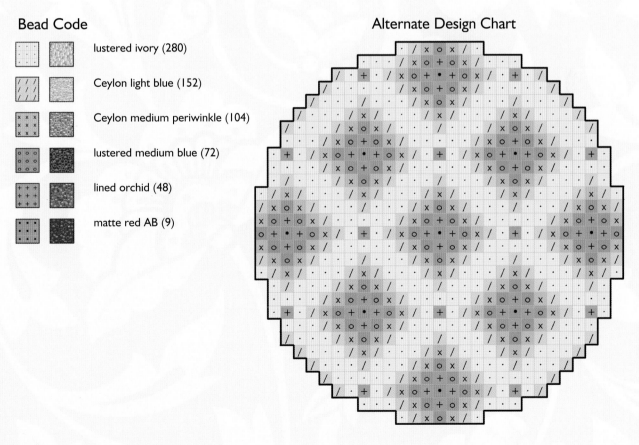

27

Alternate Design Chart

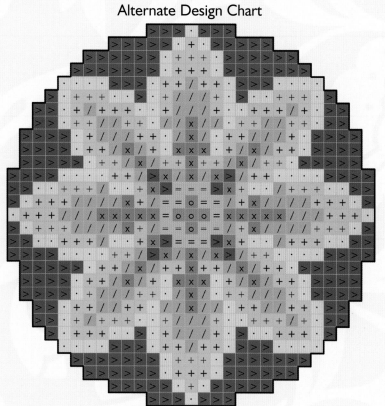

Bead Code

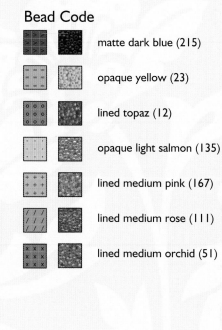

matte dark blue (215)

opaque yellow (23)

lined topaz (12)

opaque light salmon (135)

lined medium pink (167)

lined medium rose (111)

lined medium orchid (51)

Alternate Design Chart

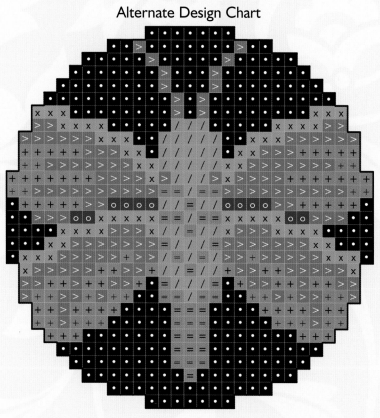

Bead Code

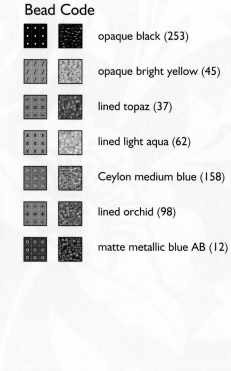

opaque black (253)

opaque bright yellow (45)

lined topaz (37)

lined light aqua (62)

Ceylon medium blue (158)

lined orchid (98)

matte metallic blue AB (12)

Bird with Berries Ornament

This design is stitched on #18 interlock canvas, using 15/0 seed beads. It may also be stitched on #14, #16, or #18 interlock canvas.

Stitch count: 47 x 47

Materials required:

Beads:
  6/0 seed beads, opaque medium green (2)
  8/0 seed beads, opaque red (8)
  11/0 seed beads, metallic gold (2)
  15/0 seed beads:
    Ceylon cream (100)
    Ceylon light blue (95)
    Ceylon salmon (254)
    lined pale lavender (120)
    lined topaz (31)
    matte dark aqua AB (190)
    matte metallic bronze (121)
    metallic gold (493)
    opaque dark amethyst (68)
    opaque dark brown (33)
    opaque dark green (97)
    opaque light amethyst (97)
    opaque medium blue (56)
    opaque medium green (212)
    opaque red (338)

Misc:
  Fabric for backing, 4" square
  #18 interlock canvas, 4" square
  Needles
  Scissors

Instructions:

1. Refer to Photo 1. Stitch as charted on page 30, leaving solid red areas unbeaded.

1

Bird with Berries Ornament Chart

Bead Code

metallic gold	opaque light amethyst
Ceylon salmon	opaque dark amethyst
opaque red	matte dark aqua AB
opaque dark green	opaque medium blue
opaque medium green	Ceylon light blue
opaque dark brown	Ceylon cream
matte metallic bronze	lined topaz
lined pale lavender	

2

3

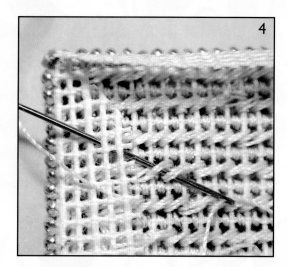

4

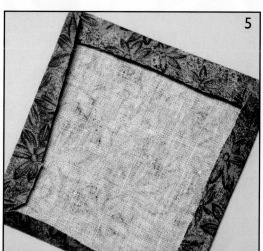

5

2. Refer to Photo 2. Sew on 8/0 seed beads, anchored with red 15/0 seed beads.

Finishing:

1. Refer to Photo 3. Trim excess canvas to ⅜". Notch corners.

2. Use trimmed canvas as a template for backing. Cut backing fabric to same size. Notch corners.

3. Refer to Photo 4. Fold excess canvas onto back side of beadwork. Slip-stitch canvas edges against back of beadwork.

4. Refer to Photo 5. Press notched excess of backing to same size as beadwork. Slip-stitch backing and beadwork together so backing does not show from beaded side.

5. Refer to Diagram A to add beaded handle. Using a doubled strand of thread for strength, bring needle out at top left of piece. Slip one opaque medium green 6/0 seed bead, one opaque red 8/0 seed bead, and one metallic gold 11/0 seed bead on needle. Slip opaque red 15/0 seed beads on needle and thread until there are 65 on the strand. Slip one metallic gold 11/0 seed bead, one opaque red 8/0 seed bead, and one opaque medium green 6/0 seed bead on needle to complete strand. Insert needle into top right of piece. Bury thread in backing.

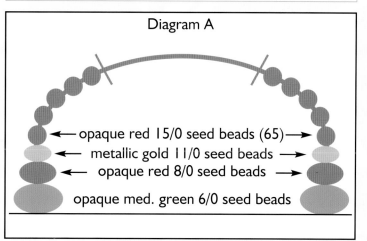

Diagram A

← opaque red 15/0 seed beads (65) →
← metallic gold 11/0 seed beads →
← opaque red 8/0 seed beads →
opaque med. green 6/0 seed beads

Blue Moon Mirror

This design is stitched on #16 duo canvas, using Delica beads. This pattern could also be used to create a brooch (2¼" diameter) by stitching on #18 interlock canvas, using 15/0 seed beads, or to make a small wall piece or ornament by stitching on #14 interlock canvas, using 11/0 seed beads.

Stitch count: 43 x 43

Materials required:
Beads:
  Delica beads:
    Ceylon light blue (43)

dyed lustered medium pink (53)
lined pale lavender (55)
lustered dark amethyst (152)
lustered dark blue (75)
matte dark brown (18)
matte dark yellow-gold AB (21)
matte emerald AB (125)
matte light gray-lavender (69)
matte light salmon (31)
matte light watermelon (87)
matte metallic dark blue (67)
matte metallic dark green (142)
matte metallic purple iris (78)
matte opaque light green (139)

matte opaque medium
　　green (180)
matte orange AB
matte pale lavender (59)
metallic gold
opaque light blue (43)
opaque lustered white (7)
opaque medium blue (30)

Misc:
　#16 duo canvas, 4" square
　Mirror backing or card-
　　board
　Mirror frame
　Needles
　Scissors
　Washable jewelry glue

Instructions:
1. Stitch as charted at right.

Finishing:
1. For use within a rounded shape such as the mirror frame, first compare finished beadwork to rounded opening for fit.

2. If necessary, fill in around edge of beadwork with beads similar in color to frame. Fill in very small spaces where white canvas may be showing with metallic gold beads.

3. Trim excess canvas to ⅜". Notch all around.

4. Glue back side of beadwork onto mirror backing, folding excess canvas onto back of backing and gluing it in place.

5. Mount finished piece in frame.

Blue Moon Mirror Chart

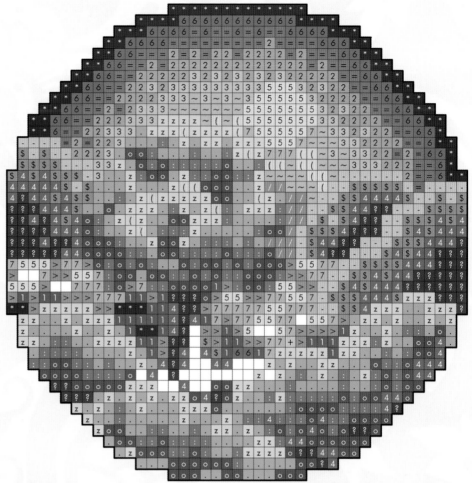

Bead Code

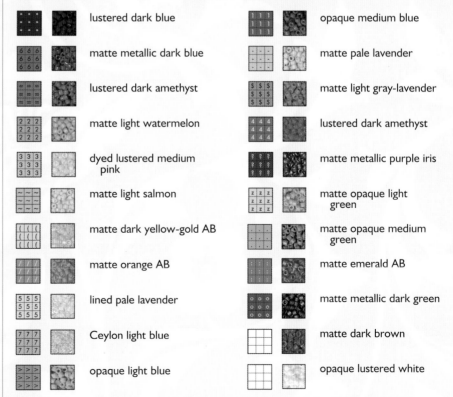

	lustered dark blue		opaque medium blue
	matte metallic dark blue		matte pale lavender
	lustered dark amethyst		matte light gray-lavender
	matte light watermelon		lustered dark amethyst
	dyed lustered medium pink		matte metallic purple iris
	matte light salmon		matte opaque light green
	matte dark yellow-gold AB		matte opaque medium green
	matte orange AB		matte emerald AB
	lined pale lavender		matte metallic dark green
	Ceylon light blue		matte dark brown
	opaque light blue		opaque lustered white

Checkered Pin

This design should be stitched on only #18 interlock canvas, using 15/0 seed beads. The finished size is 2¼" square.

Stitch count: 40 x 40

Materials required:
Beads:
  #2 bugles, matte light amethyst AB (4)
  #5 bugles, matte light amethyst AB (2)
  15mm bugles, green iris (1)
  Cobalt crystal, teardrop shape, 7mm x
    10mm (1)
  Freshwater pearls, 4mm, good quality (4)
  6/0 seed beads, metallic gold (3)
  15/0 seed beads:
    lined pale green AB (110)
    lined light yellow (116)
    lustered cream (272)
    lustered light green (96)
    metallic gold (272)
    opaque black (272)
    opaque cobalt blue (57)
    opaque dark amethyst (40)
    opaque light amethyst (26)
    opaque periwinkle blue (68)
    opaque turquoise (108)

Misc:
  #18 interlock canvas, 4" square
  Leather or ultrasuede for backing, 4" square
  Lightweight cardboard for backing
  Needles
  Pin backing
  Scissors
  Washable jewelry glue

Instructions:
1. Stitch as charted on opposite page, leaving white areas at center unbeaded.

2. For flower, sew on crystal (see photo detail at right). Fill in around crystal with pearls on both sides, then sew on three 6/0 seed beads, anchored with opaque cobalt blue 15/0 seed beads.

3. Refer to Photo 1. For flower stem, sew on 15mm bugle directly beneath crystal. Refer to Photo 2. Sew #2 bugles, both on same thread, at both sides of each leaf area. Sew #5 bugles between each set of #2 bugles; allow longer bugle to remain raised above smaller bugles.

Finishing:

1. Trim excess canvas to ⅜". Notch corners.

2. Cut cardboard to same size as beadwork. Glue back side of beadwork onto cardboard, folding excess canvas onto back of cardboard, then gluing it in place.

3. Use glued piece as a template to cut backing from leather. Glue leather onto back of piece.

4. Sew pin backing in place through all layers, taking care not to allow stitches to show on front.

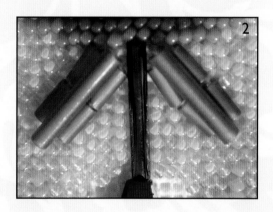

Checkered Pin Chart

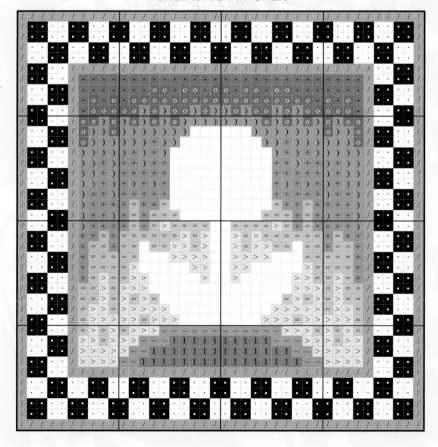

Bead Code

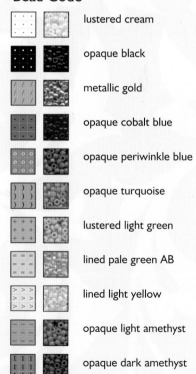

	lustered cream
	opaque black
	metallic gold
	opaque cobalt blue
	opaque periwinkle blue
	opaque turquoise
	lustered light green
	lined pale green AB
	lined light yellow
	opaque light amethyst
	opaque dark amethyst

This piece is intended to be stitched on only #16 duo canvas, using Delica beads. The design should stitch up to the size of the template.

Stitch count: 74 x 151

Materials required:
Beads:
   Delica beads:
      matte black (3786)
      matte metallic light gold or silver (2842)
      metallic bright gold (2832)
      metallic bronze iris (2746)
   15/0 seed beads for optional lace:
      matte black (100 gram package)

Misc:
   Black satin fabric for lining, 12" x 14"
   Dressmaker's pins
   #16 duo canvas, 7" x 12" (2)
   Needles
   Paper
   Scissors

Instructions:
1. Before stitching, fit collar to wearer. To do this, make two traced copies of Evening Collar Template on page 39. Cut off excess paper. Tape seam edges together at center back and try on paper collar. Front edges should rest approximately ¼" apart from each other. Collar should not sit tightly against neck, but instead sit just slightly below, near collarbone. If it is too large, trim off a few rows along seam line. If it is too small, add a few rows. Do not adjust at center front.

2. Stitch as charted on pages 40–41 for right side of collar. Stitch left side of collar in mirror image of the first side stitched.

Finishing:
1. Trim excess canvas on both left and right collar pieces to ⅜" all around except at center back, which should have a ¼" seam allowance. Sew collar pieces together at back seam. Press back seam allowance open and flat against back of beadwork.

2. Refer to Photo 1. Notch all around. Refer to Photo 2. Press notched canvas excess against back side of beadwork, then secure with slip stitches.

3. Use collar as a template for lining. Cut lining fabric ⅜" larger all around than beadwork. Notch all around. Press notched excess so lining is same size as beadwork. Refer to Photo 3. Slip-stitch lining and beadwork together so lining does not show from beaded side.

Note: If any white canvas shows after joining the lining and the beadwork, use a permanent black or metallic gold marking pen to color the visible canvas. Be certain the pen you use is labeled "permanent" to avoid having the color run.

4. Refer to Photo 4 and Diagram A. Using dressmaker's pins, mark around outer edge of collar at ⅜" intervals. Make any adjustments at center back. Starting at the center on both sides and working toward center back, sew on each loop of beads at marked intervals.

5. Bury excess thread in lining fabric of collar when finished.

3

4

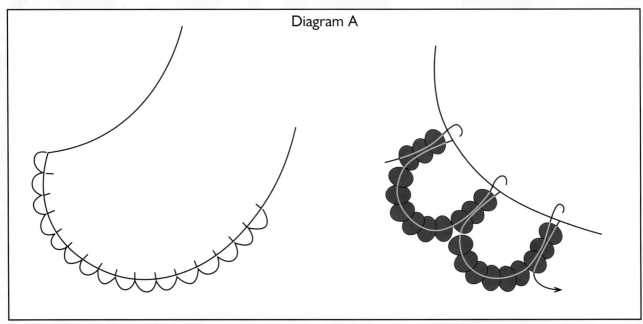

Diagram A

Bead Code

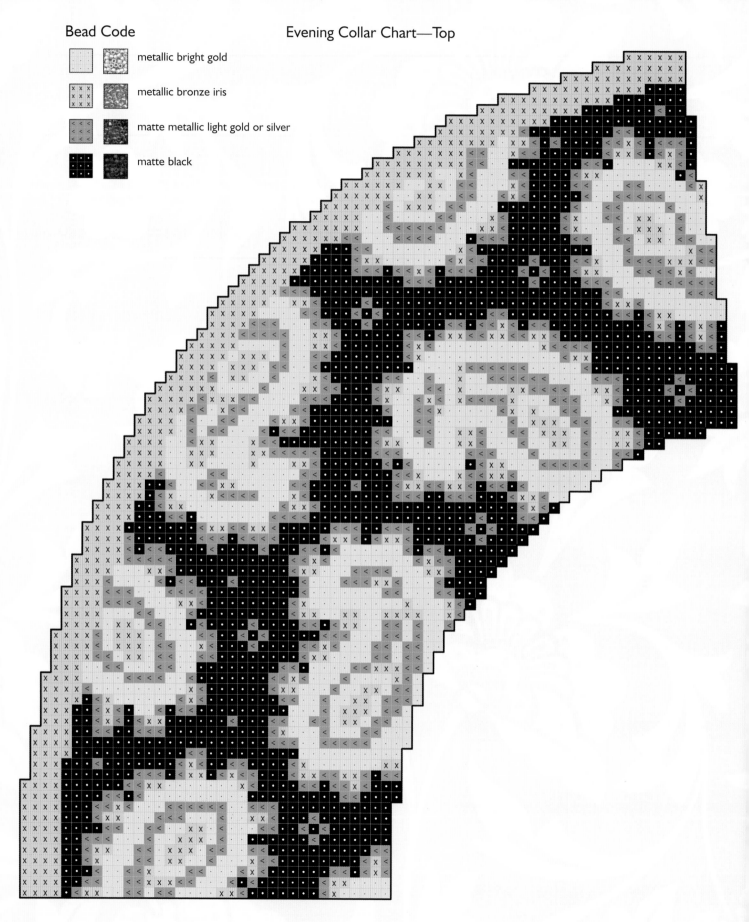

- metallic bright gold
- metallic bronze iris
- matte metallic light gold or silver
- matte black

Evening Collar Chart—Middle (connect at bottom-left bead of "Top")

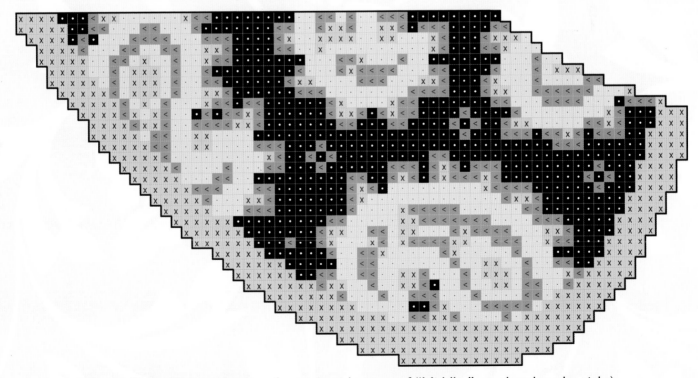

Evening Collar Chart—Bottom (connect at bottom of "Middle," one bead to the right)

Holly Heart Ornament

This design is stitched on #18 interlock canvas, using 14/0 seed beads.

Stitch count: 34 x 34

Materials required:
Misc:
Felt for backing: dark green, 4" square
#18 interlock canvas: 3" square
Jewelry glue
Needles
Satin ribbon, ⅛"-wide: red, 8"-long (2)
Scissors

Beads:
  #2 bugle beads: silver-lined gold (50)
  14/0 seed beads:
   cream (5);
   dark green (100);
   light green (75);
   medium green (100);
   medium pink (35);
   metallic gold (75);
   pale pink (6);
   red (40)

Holly Heart Ornament Chart

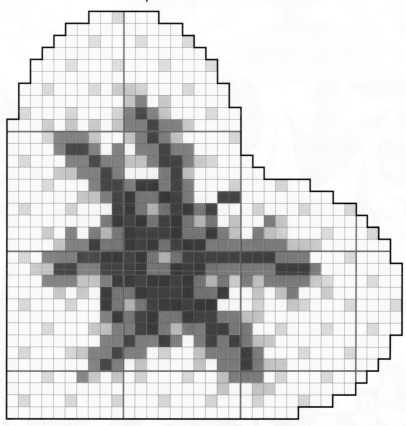

Bead Code

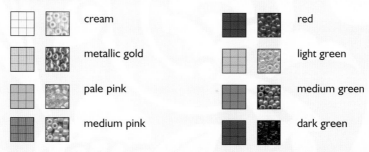

cream

metallic gold

pale pink

medium pink

red

light green

medium green

dark green

Instructions:
1. Stitch as charted above.

Finishing:
1. Trim excess canvas to ⅜". Notch all around.

2. Fold and press excess canvas against back side of beadwork.

3. Use pressed beadwork as template for backing. Cut two pieces of felt to same size and shape. Trim one piece of felt ⅛" all around for padding.

4. Sew one end of one piece of ribbon to wrong side of beadwork at each curve of heart.

5. Layer padding felt between wrong side of beadwork and backing felt. Using needle and dark green thread, slip-stitch backing felt to beadwork, enclosing padding felt and ribbons ends.

6. Sew a row of bugle beads all around edge of heart-shaped ornament. When bugle beads are in place, backtrack through all the bugle beads to position them more firmly. Bury excess thread in ornament and trim it close.

7. Tie ribbon ends in bow and trim as needed. Note: A dot of glue on the knot will help keep the bow intact when hanging it.

This design is stitched on #18 interlock canvas, using 15/0 seed beads. It would be equally attractive if stitched, using either 11/0 seed beads or Delica beads on the appropriate mesh of canvas.

The background on the model is stitched using wool. It may, of course, be stitched using beads as well; the amount needed for the background color is listed as an optional material.

Stitch count: 162 x 128

Materials required:
Beads:
  15/0 seed beads:
    Ceylon light sapphire (504)
    color of choice for background (optional)
      (6986)
    lined blue-purple (224)
    lined pale lavender (125)
    lined salmon (1493)
    lustered dark red (1361)
    matte bronze (422)
    matte light olive (1003)
    matte light seafoam green (585)
    matte medium green AB (1493)
    medium blue AB (430)
    opaque black (1204)
    opaque brown (839)
    opaque cream (429)
    opaque dark green (1547)
    opaque lustered red (799)
    opaque pale salmon (1292)

Misc:
  Dressmaker's pins
  Fabric for backing and mounting, coordinating
    color, 13½" x 17½" (2)
  #18 interlock canvas, 10" x 13"
  Needles
  Pencil
  Persian wool, single ply:
    cream (60 yards)
    lavender (12 yards)
  Pillow form, 12" x 16"
  Premade fabric fringe, 1½ yards
  Scissors
  Zipper, matching color, 14"

Instructions:
1. Stitch as charted on pages 46–49.

Finishing:
1. Reshape beadwork if necessary. Trim excess canvas to ½".

2. Place mounting fabric on work surface, then center trimmed beadwork over it. Place a pin in fabric at each corner of beadwork. Remove beadwork.

3. Use pins and pencil to lightly draw a rectangle.

4. Refer to Photo 1, right. Measure ½" in from the pencil lines, then trim away the inside of rectangle.

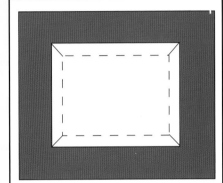

5. Clip each corner. Turn fabric under along pencil lines and press flat.

6. Place beadwork on work surface, then position rectangular opening of trimmed mounting fabric over beadwork. Baste beadwork and fabric together, then sew them together ⅛" from turned fabric edge.

7. Position fringe along seam line, gathering slightly at corners to accommodate the turn. Hand-sew fringe in place.

8. With right sides together, sew beaded piece to backing fabric with a ¾" seam allowance along sides and top, leaving bottom open. Notch corners to facilitate turning. Turn stitched pillow case right side out.

9. Insert zipper along bottom edge, following manufacturer's directions. Insert pillow form.

10. Position fringe around outer edge, gathering slightly at corners to accommodate the turn. Baste in place, avoiding sewing over zipper. Hand-sew fringe in place.

Bead Code

 opaque cream

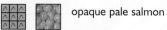 opaque pale salmon

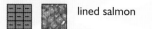 lined salmon

opaque lustered red

lustered dark red

opaque brown

lined pale lavender

Ceylon light sapphire

medium blue AB

lined blue-purple

matte light olive

matte bronze

matte light seafoam green

matte medium green AB

opaque dark green

opaque black

Floral Pillow Chart—Top Left

Floral Pillow Chart—Top Left

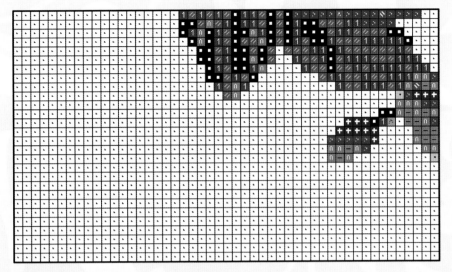

Floral Pillow Chart—Bottom Left

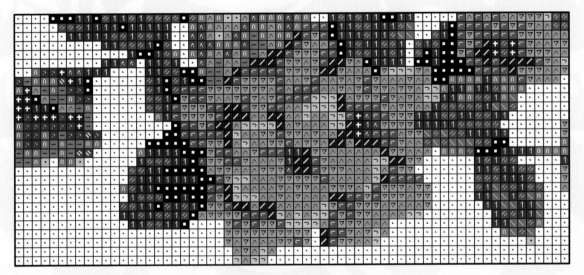

Floral Pillow Chart—Bottom Middle

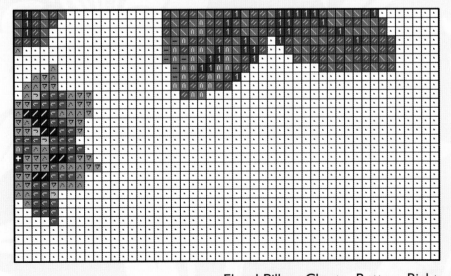

Floral Pillow Chart—Bottom Right

49

Flower Basket

This design is stitched on #16 interlock canvas, using Delica beads. However, it can be stitched on any size canvas, using the appropriate size of seed bead. If you decide to stitch it on #14 interlock canvas, using 11/0 seed beads, weight will be a factor in finishing.

As shown here, there is no cardboard lining to stiffen the piece. A cardboard lining would be required if 11/0 seed beads are used, though it need not fit the edges exactly in the upper area where there are small curves. It can simply be an approximate fit to the beadwork.

Stitch count: 86 x 91

Materials required:
Beads:
  Delica beads:
    dyed matte cranberry (341)
    dyed matte purple (227)
    lustered medium amethyst AB (273)
    matte black (282)
    matte chartreuse AB (114)
    matte cream (532)
    matte dark red (328)
    matte light blue AB (430)
    matte light turquoise green (152)
    matte medium rose (486)
    matte metallic dark green (186)
    matte metallic green AB (364)
    matte old rose (707)
    matte olive (207)
    matte opaque dark blue (540)
    matte opaque salmon (431)
    matte orange (58)
    matte pale rose (440)
    matte periwinkle (197)
    matte red AB (461)
    purple iris (97)

Misc:
  #16 duo canvas, 9" x 10"
  Leather or suede for backing, 9" square
  Metallic gold cord, ⅛" diameter, 10"
  Needles
  Scissors
  Washable jewelry glue

Instructions:
1. Stitch as charted on pages 52–53.

Finishing:
1. Reshape beadwork if necessary.

2. Trim excess canvas to ⅜". Notch convex curves and clip concave curves to facilitate turning canvas edges under, taking care to avoid cutting any beading threads.

3. Refer to Photo 1. Press excess canvas to back side of beadwork, using tweezers to position each small section if necessary. Run a thin line of glue to secure excess canvas onto stitching threads.

4. Use glued piece as a template to cut backing from leather. Position each end of cord at top left and right on back side of beadwork, then glue in place. Glue leather onto back of piece.

Note: The finished beadwork was temporarily adhered to the front of this covered binder for display purposes only.

Bead Code

 matte cream

 matte pale rose

 matte opaque salmon

 matte red AB

 matte dark red

 matte light blue AB

 matte periwinkle

 matte opaque dark blue

 matte orange

 matte old rose

 matte medium rose

 dyed matte cranberry

 lustered medium amethyst AB

 dyed matte purple

 purple iris

 matte light turquoise green

 matte metallic green AB

 matte metallic dark green

 matte black

 matte chartreuse AB

 matte olive

Flower Basket Chart—Left

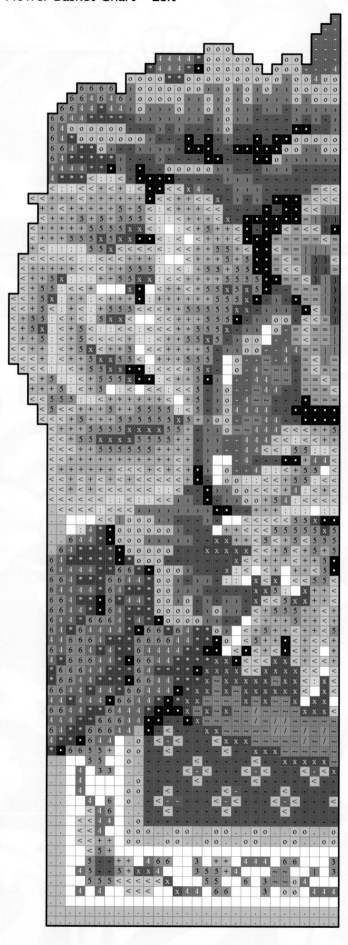

Hiroshige Camellias

This design is stitched on #18 interlock canvas, using 15/0 seed beads.

This piece was inspired by a wooden block print created by the 19th century Japanese print artist, Hiroshige, whose nature studies are well known for their beautiful colors and precise execution.

Stitch count: 72 x 108

Materials required:
Beads:
  15/0 seed beads:
    Ceylon light green (408)
    Ceylon light yellow (1302)
    lined aqua (448)
    lined light tan (97)
    lined lustered tan (210)
    lined topaz (651)
    lustered ivory (250)

    matte light topaz AB (137)
    matte medium sapphire AB (1127)
    matte transparent pink (149)
    opaque brown (751)
    opaque dark amethyst (206)
    opaque light amethyst (194)
    opaque lustered dark blue (602)
    opaque lustered light green (250)
    opaque lustered red (385)
    opaque medium green (277)

Misc:
  #18 interlock canvas, 7" x 10"
  Needles
  Scissors

Instructions:
1. Stitch as charted on pages 55–56.

Finishing:
1. Frame or finish as desired.

Bead Code

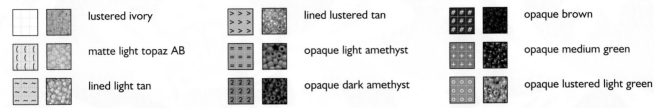

	lustered ivory
	matte light topaz AB
	lined light tan

	lined lustered tan
	opaque light amethyst
	opaque dark amethyst

	opaque brown
	opaque medium green
	opaque lustered light green

Hiroshige Camellias Chart—Top

Bead Code

 matte transparent pink

 opaque lustered red

opaque lustered dark blue

 matte medium sapphire AB

 lined aqua

Ceylon light green

 lined topaz

Ceylon light yellow

Hiroshige Camellias Chart—Bottom

56

Although this design was created to be used as an eyeglass case, it could also be set on a table to hold eating utensils or small gifts for guests. Stitch the design on #14 interlock canvas, using 11/0 seed beads. The finished size is 4" x 7".

Stitch count: 53 x 99

Materials required:
Beads:
11/0 seed beads:
    Ceylon mint green (865)
    dark amethyst (548)
    light pink (360)
    opaque dark green (651)
    opaque gold (553)
    opaque matte rose (293)
    opaque medium green (191)
    opaque orange (232)
    opaque red (825)
    opaque royal blue (761)

Misc:
#14 interlock canvas, 7" x 10"
Lightweight quilt batting or soft felt, 5" x 8"
Needles
Satin fabric for lining, 5" x 8" (2)
Scissors
Velvet fabric for backing, 5" x 8"

Instructions:
1. Stitch as charted on opposite page.

Finishing:
1. Reshape beadwork if necessary.

2. Refer to Diagram A. Trim excess canvas to ⅜". Clip corners diagonally.

3. Use trimmed beadwork as a template for lining and backing. Cut one piece from backing fabric and two pieces from lining fabric.

4. Refer to Diagram B. Turn edges of beadwork under and press so raw canvas is not visible.

5. Fold and press flat edges of backing and lining pieces at ⅜". Sew edges in place with small invisible stitches. Note: Make certain edges are pressed to napless side on velvet and to dull side on satin.

6. Use pressed backing as a template to cut lightweight quilt batting.

7. Refer to Diagram C. Place backing and one piece of lining with wrong sides together. Insert piece of lightweight quilt batting between backing and lining layers. Slip-stitch lining and backing together.

8. Place remaining piece of lining and beadwork with wrong sides together. Slip-stitch lining and beadwork together.

9. Refer to Diagram D. Place each assembled piece with lining sides together. Sew sides and bottom together with small invisible stitches, leaving top open (the stitches shown in the corner of the diagram are exaggerated). Strengthen corners with extra stitches.

Diagram A	Diagram B

Diagram C	Diagram D
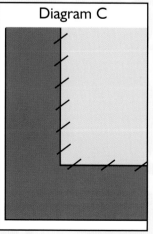	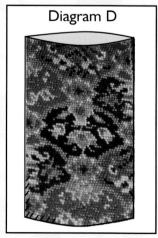

Jeweled Botanicals Chart

Bead Code

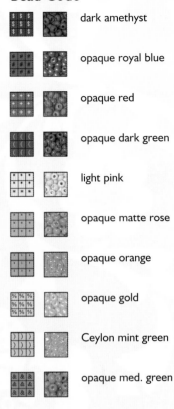

dark amethyst

opaque royal blue

opaque red

opaque dark green

light pink

opaque matte rose

opaque orange

opaque gold

Ceylon mint green

opaque med. green

Bead Code

This design should be stitched on a 6" x 10" piece of #18 interlock canvas, using 15/0 seed beads.

  opaque ivory (738)

 opaque light salmon (774)

 lined topaz (674)

matte light olive (662)

opaque medium blue (1005)

 lined medium rose (1304)

 opaque dark red (1467)

 matte dark blue (1172)

matte medium green AB (332)

Alternate Design Chart—Top

60

Alternate Design Chart—Bottom

Jeweled Purse

This design is stitched on #18 interlock canvas, using 15/0 seed beads. It is designed to fit a standard 3" purse frame. Note that the front and back designs are different; the front coordinates with the Jeweled Botanicals on pages 57–59, which is stitched using 11/0 seed beads of similar colors.

Stitch count: 81 x 68

Note: Bead counts are given separately for the front and back of the piece.

Materials required:

Beads:

15/0 seed beads for back:
- lined salmon (350)
- lined topaz (250)
- matte dark blue (408)
- matte light amethyst AB (590)
- matte light seafoam (1314)
- matte pale rose (549)
- matte red (479)
- opaque dark amethyst (591)
- opaque dark green (295)
- opaque medium seafoam (160)

15/0 seed beads for front:
- lined salmon (292)
- lined topaz (350)
- matte dark blue (570)
- matte light amethyst AB (358)
- matte light seafoam (1024)
- matte pale rose (455)
- matte red (557)
- opaque dark amethyst (579)
- opaque dark green (557)
- opaque medium seafoam (244)

Misc:
- #18 interlock canvas, 8" square (2)
- Needles
- Purse frame, brass, 3"
- Satin fabric for lining, 8" square (2)
- Scissors
- Silk cord, ¼" diameter

Instructions:

1. Stitch each side as charted on pages 64–65.

Finishing:

1. Reshape beadwork if necessary.

2. Refer to Photo 1. Trim excess canvas to ⅜". Notch convex curves and clip concave curves to facilitate turning canvas edges under, taking care to avoid cutting any beading threads.

3. Use trimmed beadwork as a template for lining. Cut two pieces from lining fabric.

4. Refer to Photo 2. Sew darts at lower corners of each lining piece. Place lining pieces with right sides together, then sew around two sides and bottom edge, matching darts.

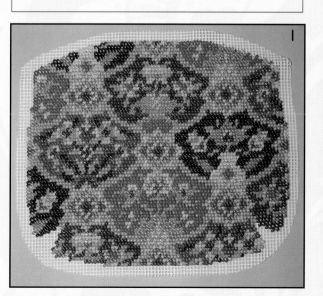

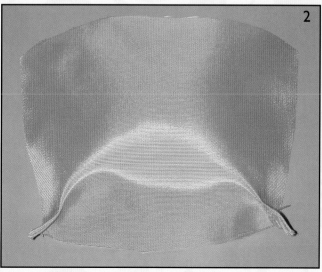

5. Press notched canvas excess against back side of each piece of beadwork. Hand-sew darts at lower corners.

6. Place beadwork pieces with wrong sides together, then slip-stitch two sides and bottom edge together.

Bead Code

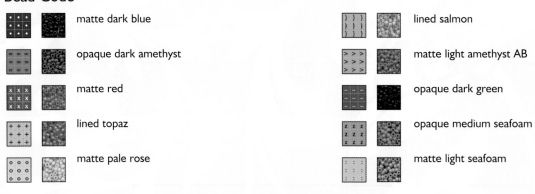

matte dark blue

opaque dark amethyst

matte red

lined topaz

matte pale rose

lined salmon

matte light amethyst AB

opaque dark green

opaque medium seafoam

matte light seafoam

Jeweled Purse Chart—Front

7. Press top edges of lining back toward raw seams. Insert lining into assembled beadwork so bottom edges meet.

8. Refer to Photo 3. Position assembled, lined piece on handle; baste beaded side in place, on front side of handle, then secure with invisible stitches. Remove basting threads. Attach lining to back side of handle.

9. Hand-sew a handle of cord to purse if desired.

Jeweled Purse Chart—Back

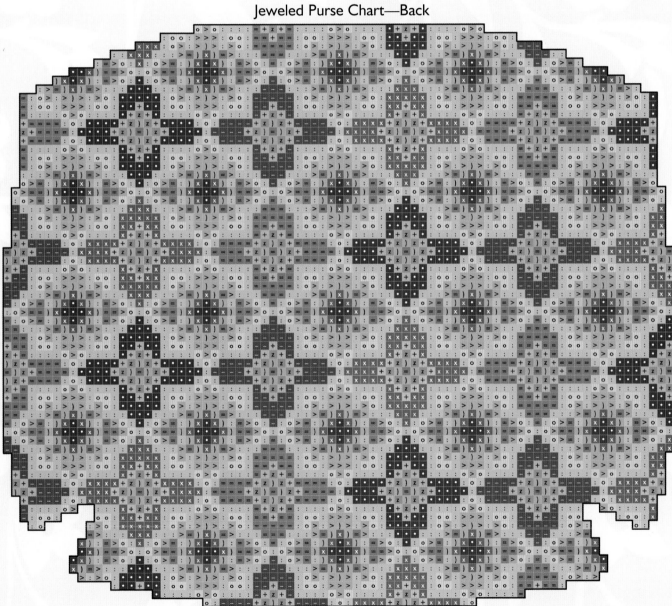

Karadja Pillow

This design is stitched on #14 interlock canvas, using 11/0 seed beads. The finished size is 11¾" square.

Stitch count: 163 x 163

Materials required:
Beads:
  11/0 seed beads:
    Ceylon light periwinkle blue (2640)
    Ceylon light salmon (2464)
    opaque brick red (856)
    opaque dark blue (3824)
    opaque dark green (3024)
    opaque lustered eggshell (7276)
    opaque red (5572)
    pearl light olive (1316)

Misc:
  Dressmaker's pins
  Fabric for backing in a coordinating color,
    45" wide, (⅔ yard)
  #14 interlock canvas, 13" square
  Needles
  Pillow form, 12" square
  Satin cord in a coordinating color, ³⁄₁₆" or ½"
    diameter (1¼ yards)
  Scissors
  Upholstery-weight piping, 1" wide (2 yards)
  Zipper, matching color, 12"

Instructions:

1. Stitch as charted on pages 68–69, turn canvas counterclockwise one quarter turn, and repeat. Continue until design is stitched four times. Note: The center lines are repeated for matching purposes, but should not be stitched twice.

Finishing:

1. Reshape beadwork if necessary. Trim excess canvas to ¾".

2. Cut two 4"-wide strips from width of backing fabric. With right sides together, join strips at one short edge to form one long strip.

3. With the seam inward, fold fabric strip in half along its entire length. Position piping at fold, then sew along entire length of strip ¼" out from the piping, taking care not to stitch too close to piping or catch piping in stitches. Gather the fabric as needed to form a long gathered tube that will be used as piping around the edge of the pillow.

4. Cut two 7½" x 13½" pieces from backing fabric. Refer to Diagram A. With right sides together, sew a seam along one long edge. Insert zipper, following manufacturer's directions. Note: This zipper will be located at the center back of the finished pillow.

5. Position piping on beadwork so its seam lies on trimmed edge of canvas and piped edge faces inward, then baste it onto right side of beadwork. Refer to Diagram B. Gathers at corners should be heavier than those on straight sides for ease in turning corners outward, and for consistent appearance with straight sides.

6. With right sides together, place zippered backing onto piped beadwork. Using small hand-stitches, sew assembly together, leaving a 1" gap at center bottom edge. Notch corners to facilitate turning. Turn entire assembly right side out through opened zipper. Pull corners out for a neat appearance.

7. Refer to Diagram C. Position cord along meeting point of beadwork and piping, tucking cord ends into gap at center bottom edge; pin into position. Sew cord in place with small invisible stitches. Slip-stitch gap closed.

8. Insert pillow form.

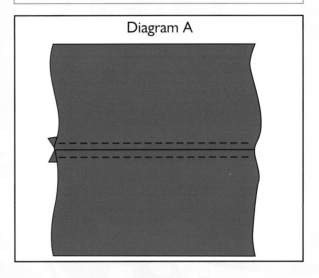

Diagram A

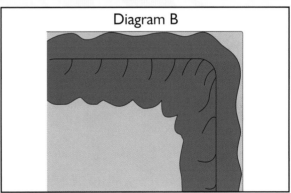

Diagram B

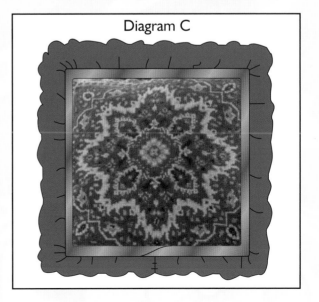

Diagram C

67

Karadja Pillow Chart—Right

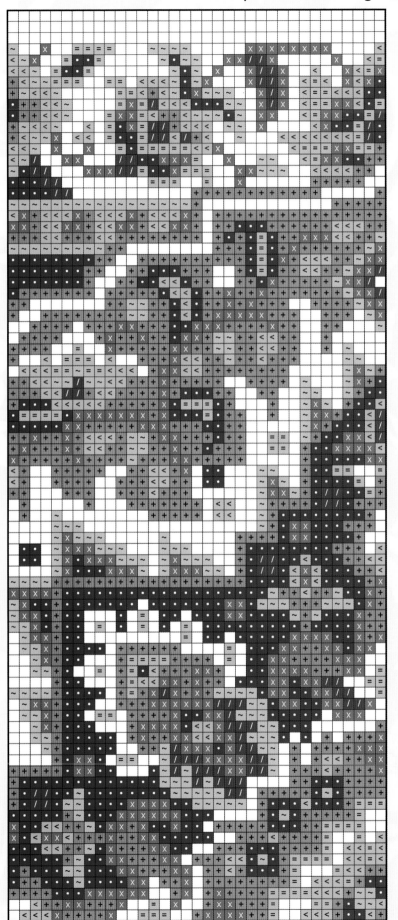

Bead Code

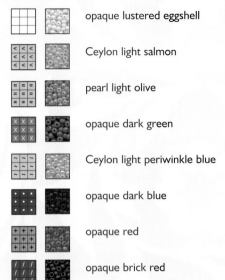

		opaque lustered eggshell
		Ceylon light salmon
		pearl light olive
		opaque dark green
		Ceylon light periwinkle blue
		opaque dark blue
		opaque red
		opaque brick red

Kilim Eyeglass Case

This design should be stitched on only #14 canvas, using 11/0 seed beads to maintain the required finished size.

Stitch count: 51 x 101

Materials required:
Beads:
  11/0 seed beads:
    matte opaque black (996)
    matte opaque chestnut brown (1011)
    matte opaque light amethyst (1355)
    matte opaque red (1789)

Misc:
  #14 interlock canvas, 6" x 10"
  Lightweight quilt batting or soft felt, 5" x 9"
  Needles
  Satin fabric for lining, 5" x 9" (2)
  Scissors
  Velvet fabric for backing, 5" x 9"

Instructions:
1. Stitch as charted on opposite page.

Finishing:
1. Refer to Jeweled Botanicals on pages 57–59 for finishing.

Kilim Eyeglass Case Chart

Bead Code

 matte opaque red

 matte opaque chestnut brown

 matte opaque light amethyst

 matte opaque black

71

This design should be stitched on only #18 interlock canvas, using 15/0 seed beads. The finished size is 2¼" x 3½".

Stitch count: 41 x 65

Materials required:
Beads:
  15/0 seed beads:
    Ceylon light blue (27)
    Ceylon light pink (60)
    lined gold (26)
    lined lavender (81)
    lined pale lavender (41)
    lined purple (38)
    lined salmon (107)
    matte dark olive (104)
    matte eggshell (727)
    opaque brick red (46)
    opaque light blue (42)
    opaque light tan (657)
    opaque lustered light pea green (18)
    opaque lustered medium green (42)
    opaque lustered medium tan (82)
    opaque medium indian blue (11)
    opaque red (76)

Misc:
  #18 interlock canvas, 4" x 6"
  Leather, suede or ultrasuede, ½" x 10" strip
  Needles
  Oval craft paper box, 2¼" x 3½" x 2" deep
  Scissors
  Washable jewelry glue

Instructions:
1. Stitch as charted on page 74.

Finishing:
1. Reshape beadwork if necessary.

2. Refer to Photo 1. Trim excess canvas to same width as flat side edge of box top.

3. Refer to Photo 2. Notch all around.

4. Refer to Photo 3. Glue back side of beadwork onto flat oval part of box top, folding notched canvas onto flat side edge of box top and gluing in place.

5. Glue leather strip around flat side edge of box top, covering notched canvas.

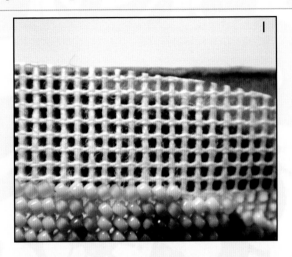

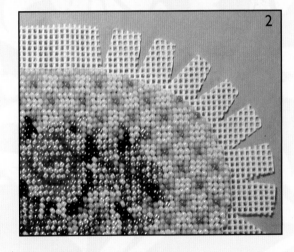

73

Oval Box Chart

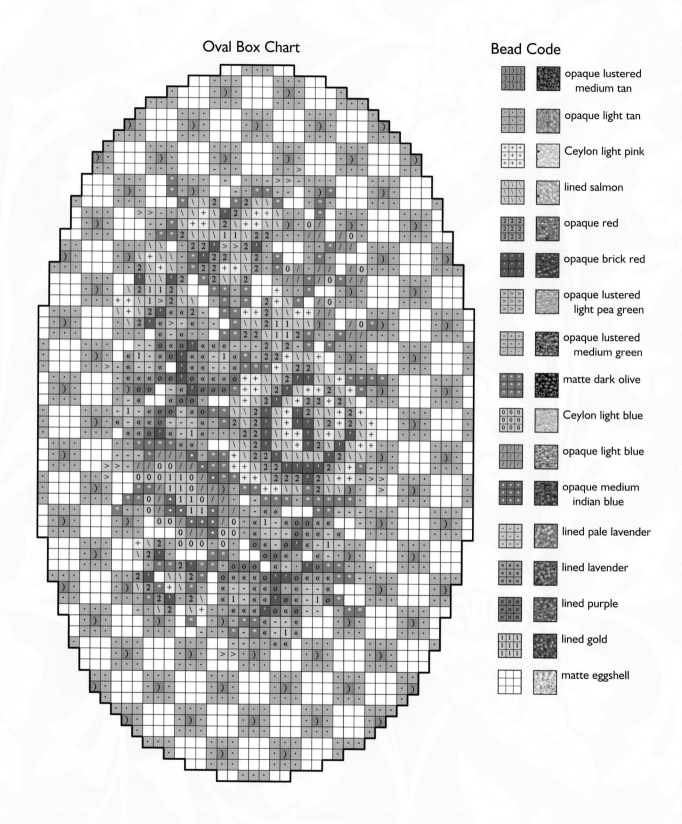

Bead Code

opaque lustered medium tan	
opaque light tan	
Ceylon light pink	
lined salmon	
opaque red	
opaque brick red	
opaque lustered light pea green	
opaque lustered medium green	
matte dark olive	
Ceylon light blue	
opaque light blue	
opaque medium indian blue	
lined pale lavender	
lined lavender	
lined purple	
lined gold	
matte eggshell	

Pearl Plant Picture

This design should be stitched on only #18 interlock canvas, using 15/0 seed beads. The finished size is 3" x 4".

Materials required:

Beads:
  #2 bugles, matte topaz AB (56)
  Freshwater pearls, 4mm, of good quality (15)
  6/0 seed beads, copper galvanized (13)
  8/0 seed beads:
    opaque cream (170)
    opaque dark amethyst (17)
  11/0 seed beads, galvanized gold (13)
  15/0 seed beads:
    dyed matte light sea green (260)
    dyed opaque dark green (250)
    matte metallic green iris (175)
    matte metallic light olive (310)
    opaque cream (425)
    opaque dark amethyst (17)
    opaque light salmon (1042)

Misc:
  Fabric for backing, 5" x 6"
  #18 interlock canvas, 5" x 6"
  Lightweight cardboard
  Needles
  Rattail cord, 5" length
  Scissors
  Washable jewelry glue

Instructions:

1. Refer to Putting the Design on the Canvas on pages 18–19. Apply Pearl Plant Picture Design on page 76 in line form or full color onto canvas.

2. Refer to Diagram A on page 76. Using opaque cream 15/0 seed beads, stitch outer line of border, directly on line. Next, stitch inner line of border. Run a single connecting thread through all beads of outer line to stabilize and smooth outer edge.

Pearl Plant Picture Design

Bead Code

		opaque light salmon
		opaque cream
		dyed opaque dark green
		matte metallic green iris
		dyed matte light sea green
		matte metallic light olive
		opaque dark amethyst

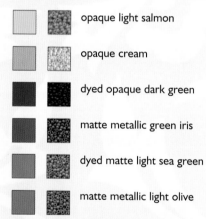

3. Refer to Diagram B. Sew on opaque cream 8/0 seed beads between inner and outer line of border. Bring needle up in lower right corner to start. Put four or six beads on needle at one time, and position beads on their sides. Refer to Diagram C. Put needle back through canvas again at the end of length of beads, then anchor short strand of beads in position on canvas with one stitch at center of strand. When all 8/0 seed beads have been sewn onto canvas, run one connecting thread through all to smooth bead line.

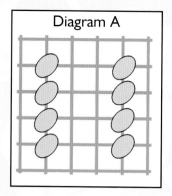

Diagram A

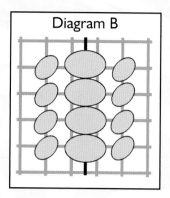

Diagram B

Diagram C

4. Refer to Photos 1 and 2. Sew on vertical strands for three greens at base of design, carrying thread from top of one strand to bottom of next on back side of canvas.

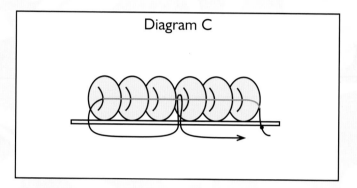

1

2

5. Refer to Photo 3. Starting at base of plant, sew on bugles in a free-form fashion, following curve of stem lines. When all beads are in place, run one connecting thread through each stem to smooth the line.

6. Refer to Photos 4 and 5. Sew on multiple-bead strands in a free-form fashion to form leaves.

7. Sew on pearls. Next, sew on copper galvanized 6/0 seed beads, anchored with gold metallic 11/0 seed beads. Finally, sew on dark amethyst 8/0 seed beads, anchored with dark amethyst 15/0 seed beads.

8. Refer to Photo 6. Fill in background. Stitch all beads that can be stitched at the proper bead-point slant, then go back and sew on beads in free-form fashion to fill in any canvas gaps.

Finishing:

1. Trim excess canvas to ⅜". Notch concave curves and trim corners.

2. Use trimmed canvas as a template for backing. Cut backing fabric to same size. Notch curves and trim corners.

3. Fold and press excess canvas against back side of beadwork.

4. Fold and press notched excess of backing to same size as beadwork.

5. Cut cardboard to ⅛" smaller than beadwork.

6. For optional hanger, cut ⅛" rattail cord to approximately 5" in length, then sew it onto either side of top edge of beadwork.

7. Layer cardboard between wrong sides of backing and beadwork. Slip-stitch backing and beadwork together.

Peony Pin

This design is stitched on #18 canvas, using 15/0 seed beads. If stitched on #16 canvas, using Delica beads, it would make a nice small pocket for a shirt front or sleeve.

Stitch count: 47 x 47

Materials required:
Beads:
#2 bugles, silver lined green AB (56)
15/0 seed beads:
  Ceylon light green (96)
  Ceylon light pink (358)
  Ceylon light sapphire (34)
  lined medium green (152)
  lined medium pink (380)
  lined pale pink (181)
  opaque brick red (134)
  opaque dark green (113)
  opaque lustered cobalt (326)
  opaque lustered medium sapphire (146)
  opaque lustered red AB (196)

Misc:
  #18 canvas, 4" square
  Cardboard for backing
  Fabric for backing, 4" square
  Needles
  Pin backing, 1¼"
  Scissors
  Washable jewelry glue

Instructions:
1. Stitch as charted on opposite page.

Finishing:
1. Trim excess canvas to ⅜". Notch corners.

2. Cut cardboard to ⅛" smaller all around than beadwork. Glue back side of beadwork onto cardboard, folding excess canvas onto back of cardboard and gluing in place.

3. Use beadwork as a template for backing. Cut backing fabric ⅜" larger all around than beadwork. Press excess fabric under so backing is same size as beadwork.

4. Position backing fabric on back of piece so it covers cardboard. Slip-stitch entire assembly together.

5. Sew bugle beads all around edge of piece, where fabric meets beadwork. Sew each bead on individually, then run one connecting thread through all bugles to smooth the line. Bury excess thread in the backing fabric.

6. Sew pin backing in place through all layers, taking care not to allow stitches to show on front.

Bead Code

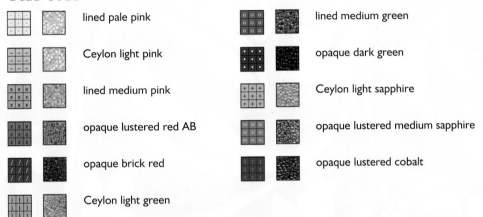

lined pale pink

Ceylon light pink

lined medium pink

opaque lustered red AB

opaque brick red

Ceylon light green

lined medium green

opaque dark green

Ceylon light sapphire

opaque lustered medium sapphire

opaque lustered cobalt

Peony Pin Chart

Bead Code

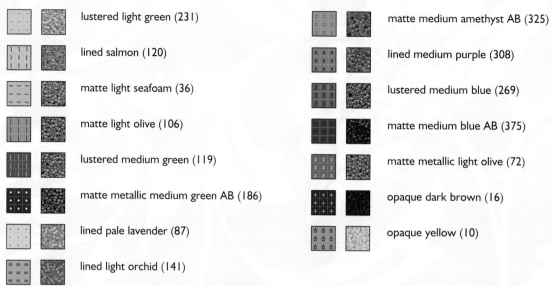

- lustered light green (231)
- lined salmon (120)
- matte light seafoam (36)
- matte light olive (106)
- lustered medium green (119)
- matte metallic medium green AB (186)
- lined pale lavender (87)
- lined light orchid (141)

- matte medium amethyst AB (325)
- lined medium purple (308)
- lustered medium blue (269)
- matte medium blue AB (375)
- matte metallic light olive (72)
- opaque dark brown (16)
- opaque yellow (10)

Alternate Design Chart

Persian Rug Purse

This design is stitched on #18 canvas, using 15/0 seed beads. It can also be stitched on #16 duo canvas, using Delica beads and on #14 interlock canvas, using 11/0 seed beads.

Stitch counts: 81 x 73 (Body) and 81 x 25 (Flap)

Materials required:
Misc:
  Clasp (optional)
  Fabric for backing, ¼ yard
  Fabric for lining, ¼ yard
  #18 interlock canvas, 8" x 10"
  Needles
  Permanent marking pen, red
  Scissors

Beads:
  15/0 seed beads:
    black (3183)
    lustered cream (107)
    opaque brick red (166)
    opaque green (612)
    opaque light blue (319)
    opaque orange (542)
    opaque red (2619)

Instructions:
1. Stitch each piece separately as charted on pages 82–84.

Bead Code

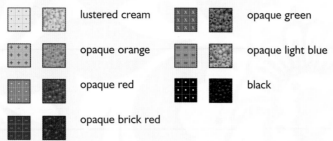

- lustered cream
- opaque orange
- opaque red
- opaque brick red
- opaque green
- opaque light blue
- black

Persian Rug Purse Chart—Flap Left

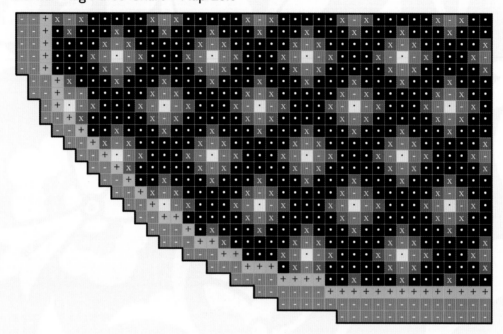

Persian Rug Purse Chart—Flap Right

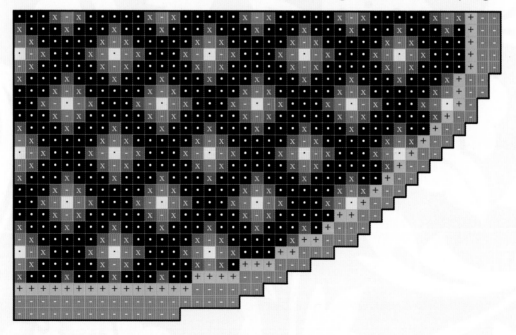

Persian Rug Purse Chart—Body Left

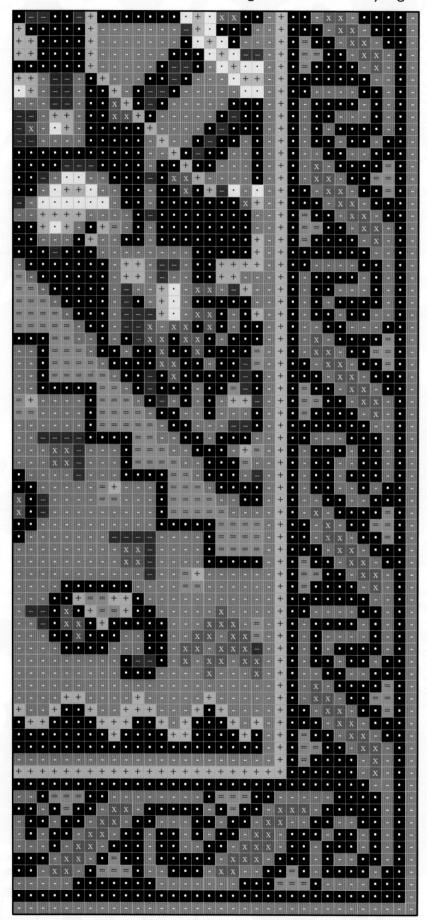

Finishing:

1. Reshape the beaded pieces if necessary.

2. Refer to Photo 1 on opposite page. Color the curved edge of the flap with permanent marking pen.

3. Refer to Photo 2 on opposite page. Trim excess canvas on both pieces to ⅜". Notch corners and curved edges.

4. Use trimmed pieces as templates for lining and backing. Cut one piece from lining fabric for flap, two pieces from lining fabric for body, and one piece from backing fabric for body.

5. Refer to Photo 3 on opposite page. Turn edges under on all pieces and press flat.

6. Refer to Photo 4 and Diagram A on opposite page. Slip-stitch edges in place.

7. Assemble flap; slip-stitch bead-work and lining together (with wrong sides together). Assemble body back; slip-stitch one lining piece and backing together (with wrong sides together). Assemble beaded body front; slip-stitch remaining lining piece and bead-work together (with wrong sides together).

8. Refer to Diagram B on opposite page. Assemble purse; slip-stitch sides and bottom with invisible stitches, then add flap so it will fold over beaded body front.

9. Following the manufacturer's instructions, add optional clasp.

1

4

2

Diagram A

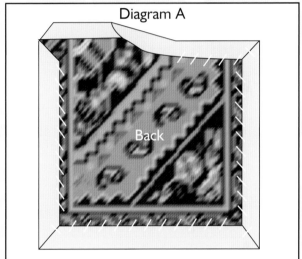

Back

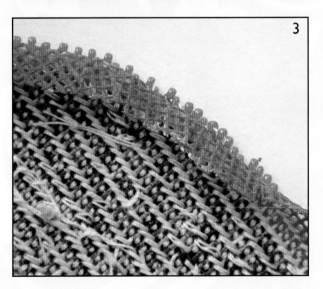

3

Diagram B

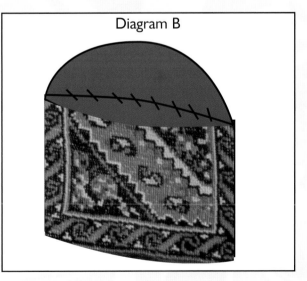

Rose Cottage

This design is stitched on #16 duo canvas, using Delica beads. The finished size is 6" in diameter.

Stitch count: 95 x 95

Materials required:
Beads:
  Delica beads:
    light pink (2046)
    maroon (740)
    medium pink (1157)
    medium rose (1095)
    white (2223)

Misc:
  Cardboard
  #16 duo canvas, 9" square
  Leather, suede or ultrasuede, maroon, 3"-wide
    strip
  Needles
  Satin cord, pink, ³⁄₁₆" or ¼" diameter (1 yard)
  Scissors
  Upholstery-weight piping, ½" to ¾" wide
    (⅔ yard)
  Washable jewelry glue

Instructions:
1. Stitch as charted on pages 87–88.

white

light pink

medium pink

medium rose

maroon

Finishing:

1. Trim excess canvas to ½". Refer to Photo 1. Notch all around to facilitate turning edges under.

2. Cut cardboard to same size as beadwork. Refer to Photo 2. Glue back side of beadwork onto cardboard, folding excess canvas onto back of cardboard and gluing in place.

3. Create fluted edge by folding leather strip in half along its entire length. Refer to Diagram A. Position piping at fold, then sew along entire length of strip, taking care not to stitch too close to piping or catch piping in stitches. Note: As you sew, pull the piping so the fabric gathers as you go.

4. Form gathered tube into a circle and trim piping so ends just meet around mounted beadwork.

5. Refer to Diagram B. Slip-stitch ends of piping together and pull ends of gathered tube together to cover piping. Note: If you have used a raveling fabric, tuck the edges under before joining together.

6. Nestle beadwork into "frame" created by covered piping to check for fit. Using a liberal amount of glue, attach beadwork to frame.

7. Glue cord around edge of beadwork with the joint meeting at bottom center. Make a bow from trim and glue in place over joint.

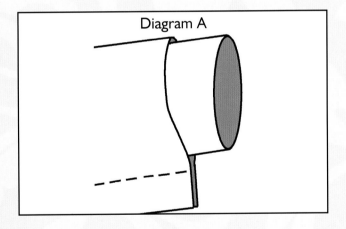

Diagram A

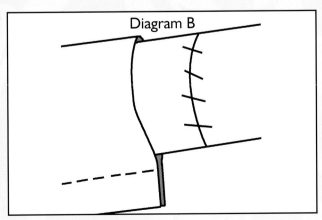

Diagram B

Rose Purse

This design is stitched on #16 duo canvas, using Delica beads. The front and the back are lined in satin and sewn together at the seams to create an ovoid envelope clutch purse.

Stitch counts: 109 x 67 (Front) and 109 x 94 (Back)

Materials required:
Misc:
  #16 duo canvas, 8" x 12"
  Needles
  Satin fabric for lining, in coordinating color,
    ½ yard
  Scissors

Beads:
  Delica beads:
    matte blue green (1479)
    matte dark emerald (1436)
    matte eggshell (932)
    matte lavender (2013)
    matte light olive AB (655)
    matte light seafoam (796)
    matte olive (800)
    matte pale lavender (2484)
    matte purple (667)
    matte red (885)
    matte salmon (1015)
    metallic gold (165)

Instructions:

1. Stitch each piece separately as charted on pages 92–94. Note: Make certain that the stitches are slanted so that when the pieces are assembled, the beads will all slant in the same direction.

Finishing:

1. Reshape beadwork if necessary.

2. Refer to Photos 1 and 2. Trim excess canvas to ⅜" on both front and back pieces. Notch convex curves and clip concave curves to facilitate turning canvas edges under, taking care to avoid cutting any beading threads.

3. Use trimmed beadwork as a template for lining. Cut one front piece and one back piece from lining fabric. Notch convex curves and clip concave curves.

4. Press notched canvas excess against back side of each piece of beadwork. Press notched excess of lining so it is same size as beadwork.

5. Refer to Photo 3. Use permanent marking pen to color edge of canvas to match lining fabric.

6. Refer to Photo 4. With wrong sides together, position each lining piece on matching beadwork, then baste together. Slip-stitch lining and beadwork together along top edge first on both pieces. If necessary, reposition lower edges for a good match, then slip-stitch bottom edges together.

7. Place assembled pieces with lining sides together so the bottom edges and sides line up. Baste pieces together approximately ½" from edge.

8. Carefully slip-stitch along the side and bottom edges. Remove all basting stitches.

9. Fold flap down over front and place a clean white paper towel over beadwork. Lightly press along fold line to shape the flap into position.

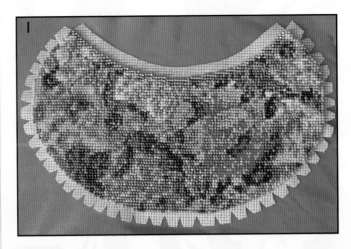

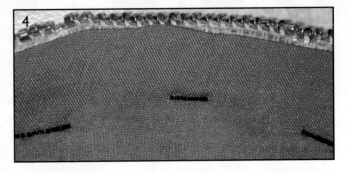

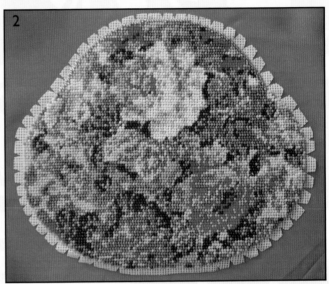

Bead Code

metallic gold

matte eggshell

matte pale lavender

matte lavender

matte purple

matte salmon

matte red

matte light seafoam

matte blue green

matte light olive AB

matte olive

matte dark emerald

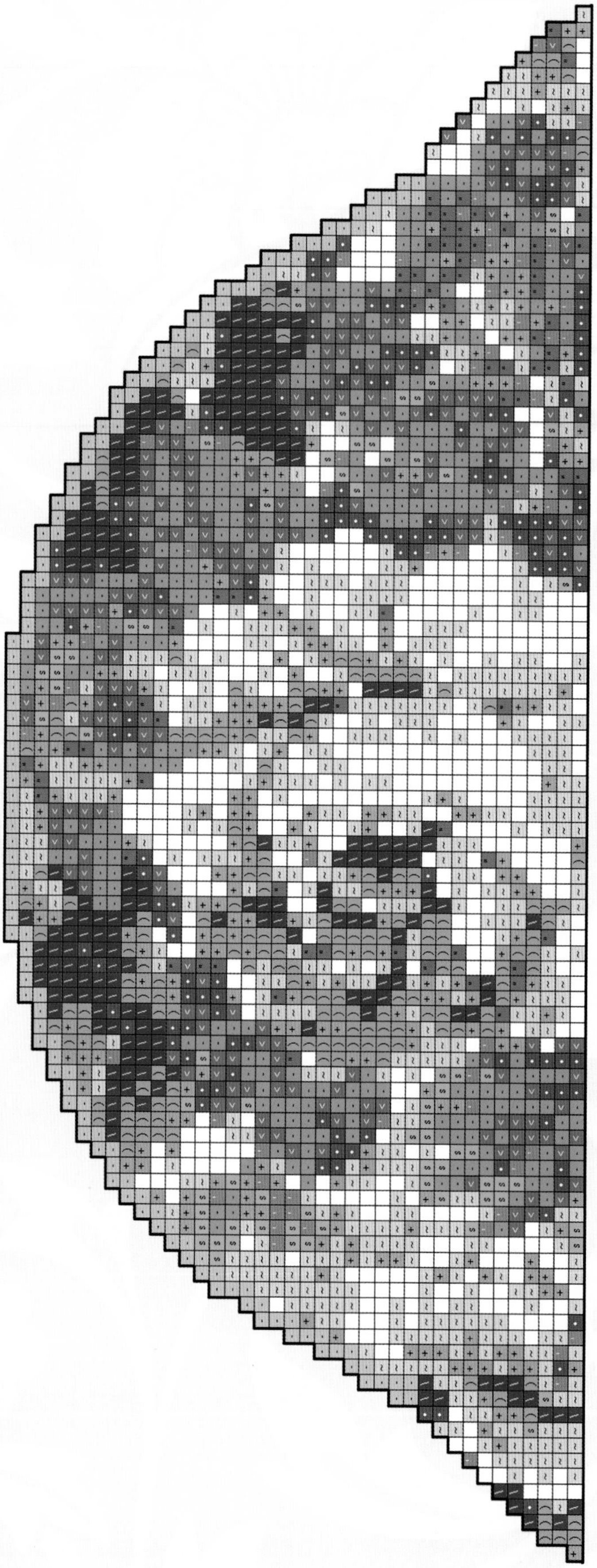

Rose Purse Chart—Back Top (with flap)

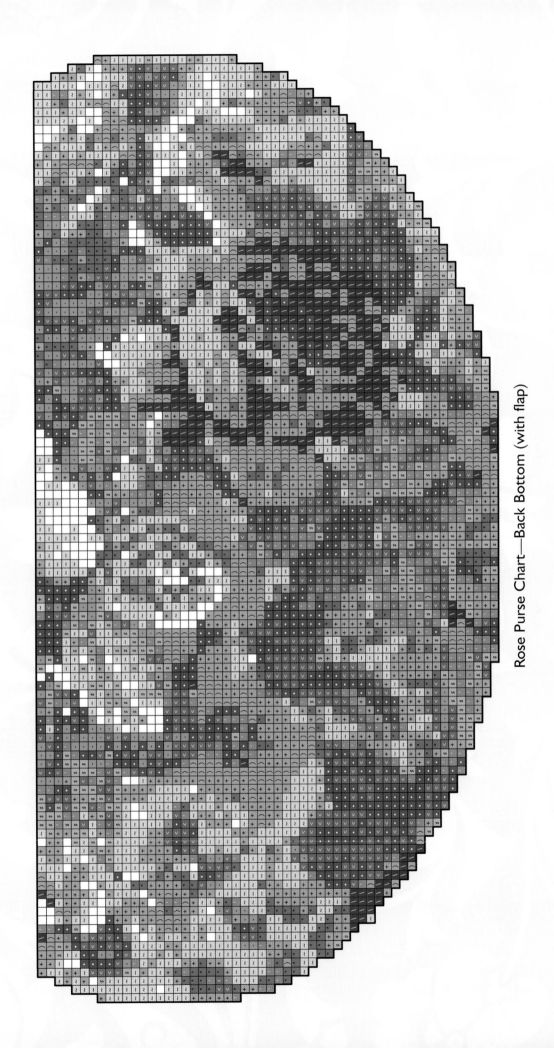

Rose Purse Chart—Back Bottom (with flap)

93

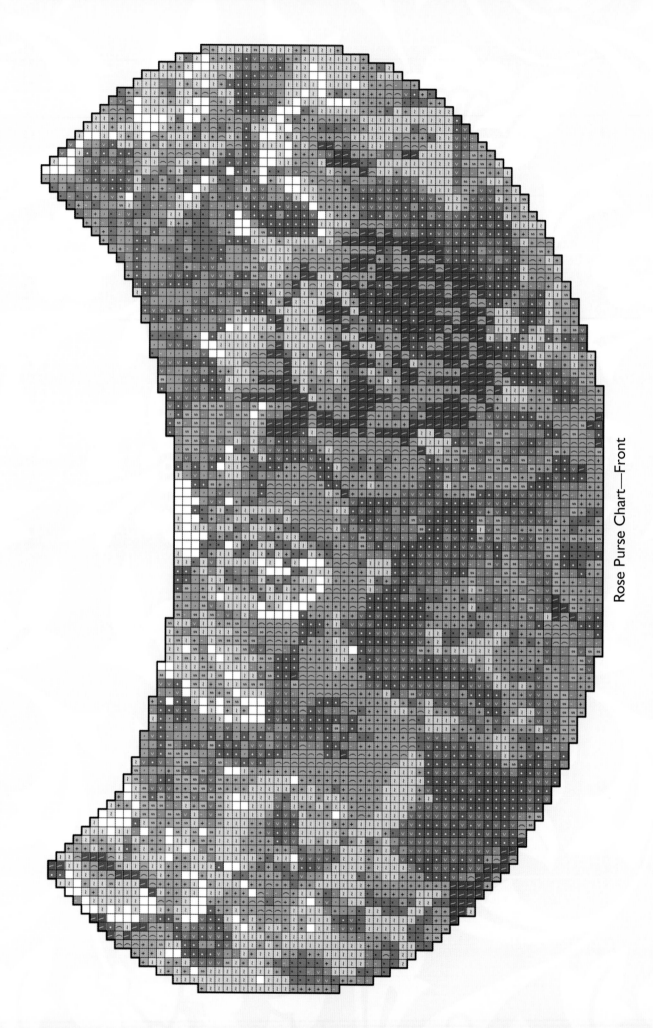

Rose Purse Chart—Front

When stitched on larger canvas, the size of this design will adapt to different sizes of scissors. As shown, stitched on #18 interlock, using 15/0 seed beads, it holds a small pair of embroidery scissors.

Stitch count: 53 x 98

Materials required:
Beads:
  8/0 seed beads:
    lustered light rose (9)
    matte light topaz (15)
  15/0 seed beads:
    Ceylon blue-green (37)
    Ceylon light gray (102)
    Ceylon sky blue (189)
    dyed opaque dark olive (170)
    lined light green (197)
    lined light salmon (100)
    lined orchid (136)
    lined pale lavender (159)
    lined peachy rose (169)
    lined rose-orchid (99)
    lined salmon (104)
    lined yellow (157)
    lustered white (291)
    matte light seafoam (170)
    matte medium blue AB (91)
    matte medium brown AB (93)
    matte medium teal green (237)
    matte opaque olive (188)
    opaque light pea green (308)
    opaque medium pea green (182)
    transparent medium green (133)

Misc:
  Fabric for backing, 6" x 9"
  Fabric for lining, 6" x 9" (2)
  #18 interlock canvas, 6" x 9"
  Needles
  Scissors

Instructions:
1. Stitch as charted on opposite page, leaving white areas with rose and topaz dots unbeaded.

2. When beadpoint is complete, sew on topaz 8/0 seed beads anchored with lined yellow 15/0 seed beads, and lustered light rose 8/0 seed beads anchored with lined peachy rose 15/0 seed beads.

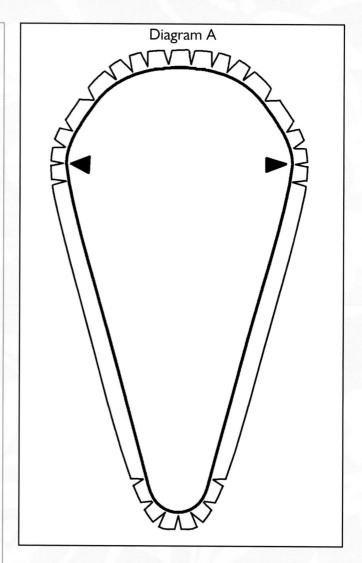
Diagram A

Finishing:
1. Refer to Diagram A. Trim excess canvas to ⅜". Notch edges as shown.

2. Use trimmed notched piece as a template for lining and backing. Cut one piece from backing fabric and two pieces from lining fabric. Notch in same manner as beadwork.

3. Turn edges of beadwork under and press so raw canvas is not visible. Repeat for one piece of lining fabric. Slip-stitch the two pieces together.

4. Sew one piece of backing and one piece of lining together (with wrong sides together) so it is same size as lined beadwork.

5. Slip-stitch assembled pieces together, with lining fabric pieces together, leaving curved top edge between arrows open.

Scissors Case Chart

Bead Code

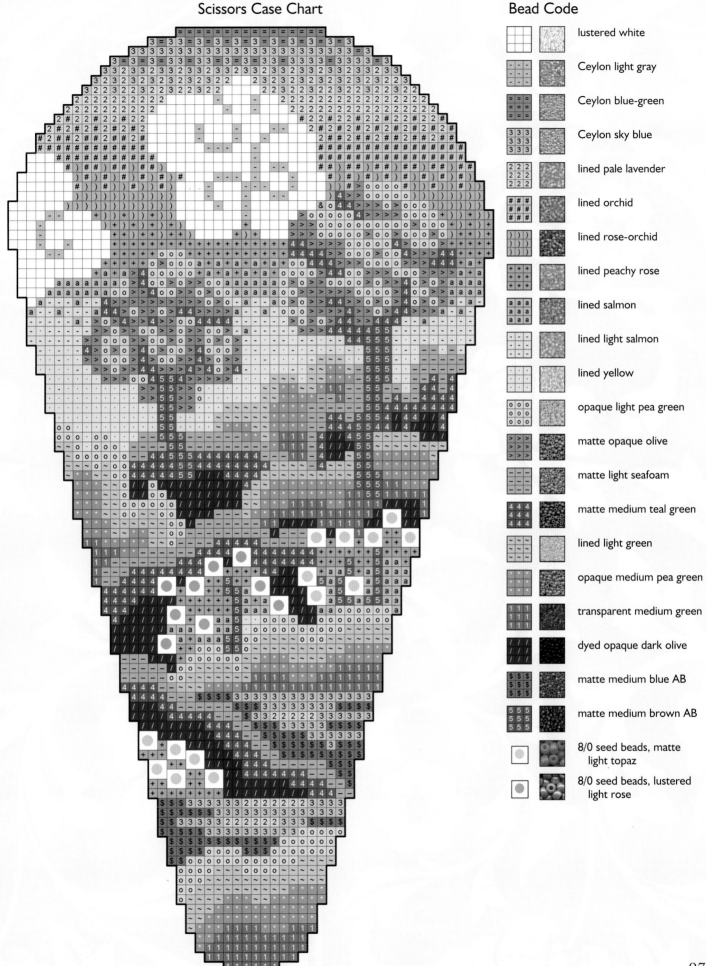

	lustered white
	Ceylon light gray
	Ceylon blue-green
	Ceylon sky blue
	lined pale lavender
	lined orchid
	lined rose-orchid
	lined peachy rose
	lined salmon
	lined light salmon
	lined yellow
	opaque light pea green
	matte opaque olive
	matte light seafoam
	matte medium teal green
	lined light green
	opaque medium pea green
	transparent medium green
	dyed opaque dark olive
	matte medium blue AB
	matte medium brown AB
	8/0 seed beads, matte light topaz
	8/0 seed beads, lustered light rose

Bead Code

		lined pale lavender (228)
		matte light lavender (398)
		opaque light amethyst (405)
		opaque dark lavender (628)
		lined pale pink (185)
		lined light orchid (419)
		lined medium rose-orchid (318)
		matte dark mauve (222)
		matte light seafoam (148)
		lustered medium green (84)
		matte bottle green (141)
		matte opaque black (247)

Tiger

This design is stitched on #18 interlock canvas, using 15/0 seed beads. The finished size is 5" x 7", which fits nicely into a standard sized frame. However, this piece may be stitched on any mesh canvas. If stitched on #14 interlock canvas, using 11/0 beads, the finished size is 6½" x 9". When stitched on #16 duo canvas, using Delica beads, the finished size is 5⅝" x 7¾". Use photo mats to increase the size to a standard frame size.

Stitch count: 90 x 126

Materials required:
Misc:
  #18 interlock canvas, 8" x 10"
  Needles
  Scissors

Beads:
15/0 seed beads:
black (1034)
lined aqua (416)
lined pale lavender-gray (1589)

lined red (29)
lined salmon (26)
opaque brick red (1156)
opaque dark brown (1800)
opaque dark gray (1563)

Bead Code

 opaque dark sapphire

 lined aqua

 opaque orchid

 opaque white

 lined pale lavender-gray

 opaque medium gray

 opaque dark gray

 black

 opaque orange

 opaque brick red

 opaque dark brown

 opaque yellow (eyes only)

 lined salmon (nose)

 lined red (nose)

Tiger Chart—Top

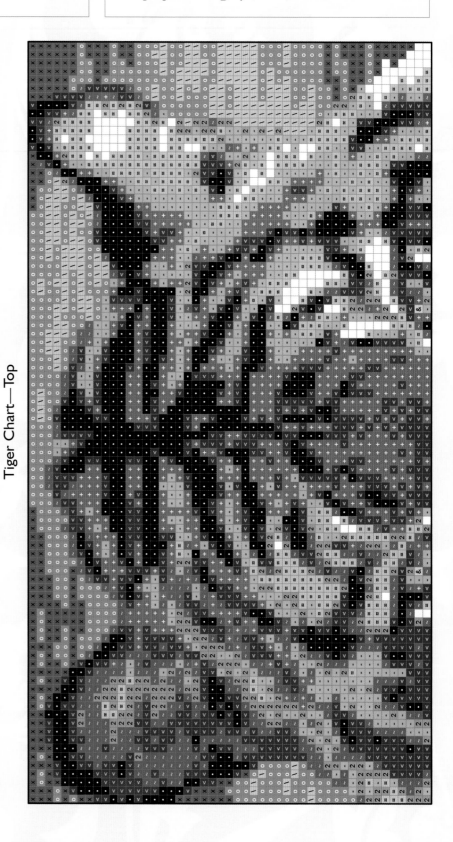

opaque dark sapphire (219)
opaque medium gray (1450)
opaque orange (1252)
opaque orchid (197)
opaque white (185)
opaque yellow (2)

Instructions:
1. Stitch as charted below and on opposite page.

Finishing:
1. Frame or finish as desired.

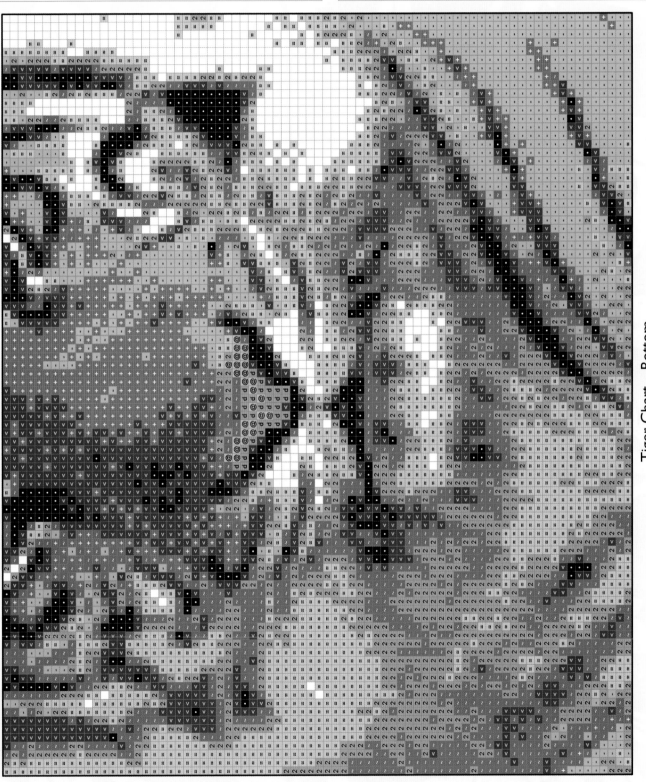

Tiger Chart—Bottom

Tree Star Necklace

This design should be worked on only #18 interlock canvas, using 15/0 seed beads in order to size the open areas correctly for the larger beads. The finished size is 1⅝" diameter.

Stitch count: 31 x 31

Materials required:

Misc:
 #18 interlock canvas, 3" square
 Leather or ultrasuede for backing, 3" square
 Lightweight cardboard for backing
 Neck chain
 Needles
 Scissors
 Washable jewelry glue

Beads:
 6/0 seed beads, matte aqua AB (10)
 8/0 seed beads, green turquoise opaque (14)
 15/0 seed beads:
  dyed dark forest green (48)
  lined blue-purple (108)
  lined orchid (71)
  lined pale peach (55)
  lined rose (50)
  lined salmon (39)
  matte blue-green AB (32)
  matte light seafoam (70)
  metallic silver (120)
  opaque dark amethyst (35)
  opaque dark brown (13)
  transparent crystal AB (5)
 Turquoise chips with heavy dark veining: 3mm x 5mm (2); 5mm x 7mm (1)

Instructions:

1. Refer to Photo 1. Stitch as charted at right, leaving white areas unbeaded.

2. Refer to Photo 2. Sew on turquoise chips, anchored with matte light seafoam 15/0 seed beads, in three lower white areas, placing larger chip in center with two smaller chips to the left and right.

3. Sew on 8/0 seed beads, anchored with matte light seafoam 15/0 seed beads, and 6/0 seed beads in upper white areas as charted.

Finishing:

1. Refer to Photo 3. Trim excess canvas to ⅜". Notch all around.

2. Cut cardboard to same size as beadwork. Glue back side of beadwork onto cardboard, folding excess canvas onto back of cardboard and gluing in place.

3. Use glued piece as a template to cut backing from leather. Glue leather onto back of cardboard.

4. Add a neck chain to create a necklace.

Tree Star Necklace Chart

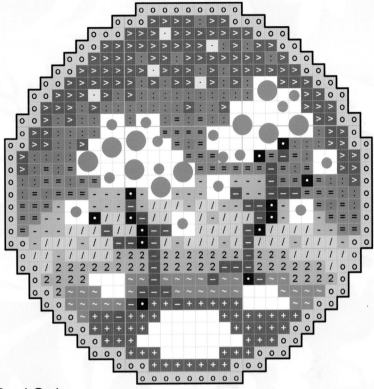

Bead Code

metallic silver		matte light seafoam
lined blue-purple		matte blue-green AB
lined orchid		dyed dark forest green
lined rose		transparent crystal AB
lined salmon		dark opaque amethyst
lined pale peach		dark brown opaque

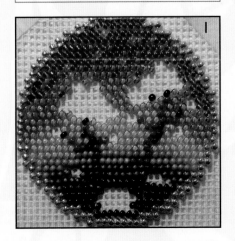

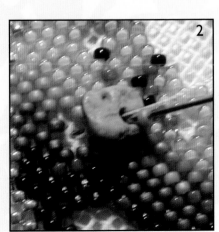

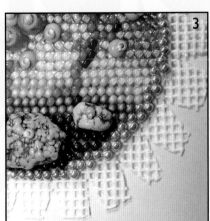

Vest Ornament

This design is stitched on #18 canvas, using 15/0 beads. It can also be stitched on #16 canvas, using Delica beads.

Stitch count: 41 x 48

Materials required:

Misc:
  #18 canvas, 4" square
  Decorative paper for backing
  Lightweight cardboard
  Needles
  Satin ribbon, ⅛" wide, red, 8" long (2)
  Scissors
  Washable jewelry glue

Beads:
  15/0 seed beads:
    Ceylon light green (256)
    lined salmon (173)
    lined yellow (570)
    matte opaque red (198)
    opaque brick red (26)
    opaque dark green (38)
    opaque light blue (133)
    opaque lustered medium green (168)
    opaque medium blue (86)

Instructions:
1. Stitch as charted on opposite page.

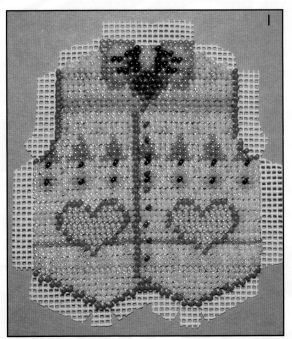

Finishing:

1. Refer to Photo 1. Trim excess canvas to ¼". Notch at corners and curves.

2. Cut cardboard to same size as beadwork. Glue back side of beadwork onto cardboard, folding excess canvas onto back of cardboard and gluing in place.

3. Glue one piece of ribbon to back side of glued piece at each shoulder.

4. Use glued piece as a template to cut backing from decorative paper. Glue paper onto back of cardboard.

5. Tie ribbon ends in bow and trim as needed.

Bead Code

	lined yellow
	lined salmon
	matte opaque red
	opaque brick red
	Ceylon light green
	opaque lustered medium green
	opaque dark green
	opaque light blue
	opaque medium blue

Vest Ornament Chart

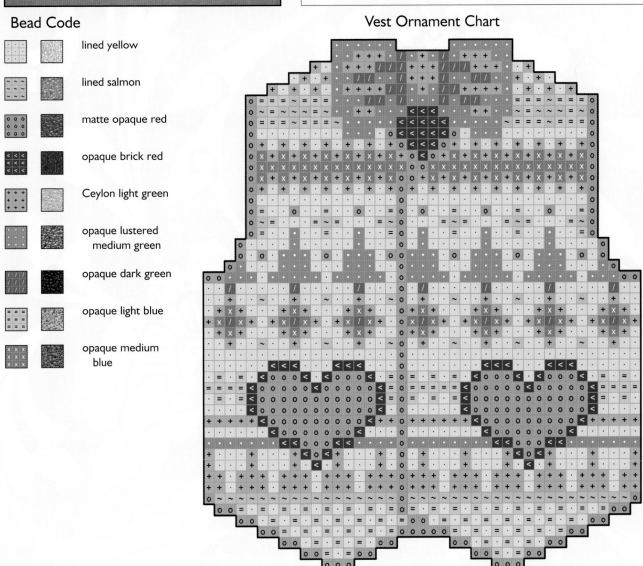

Willow in Blue Plate

This design, inspired by one on an actual plate, is stitched on #16 duo canvas, using Delica beads. The finished size is 10¾" in diameter.

Stitch count: 173 x 173

Materials required:
Beads:
  Delica beads:
    dark blue (or black) (4185)

light blue (2931)
medium blue (4172)
pale blue (4274)
white (8331)

Misc:
  #16 duo canvas, 14" square
  Foam-core board
  Needles
  Satin cord, diameter multiplied by 3.2

Scissors
Washable jewelry glue

Instructions:
1. Stitch as charted on pages 108–113.

Finishing:
1. Reshape beadwork if necessary.

2. Trim excess canvas to ¼" all around.

3. Cut a circle from foam-core board, ½" larger in diameter than beadwork.

4. Refer to Photo 1. Apply a thin, uniform coating of glue on board. Position beadwork on board, and carefully press in place. Make certain glue does not seep through to bead surface. Turn piece face-down on waxed paper and place a weight on top of it so the bond will be close. Allow glue to dry.

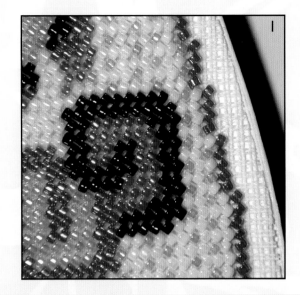

5. Glue cord around edge of beadwork with joint meeting at bottom center.

6. Unravel a short section of cord and press it with a hot iron to eliminate kinks in the fibers. Glue these fibers over cut line.

(Left) This is the actual plate that inspired the design. Just about any real or imagined scene or object is suitable for interpretation in the medium of beadpoint.

Bead Code

⊞	◼	dark blue (or black)
⊞	▨	medium blue
▤	▨	light blue
▦	▨	pale blue
☐	▨	white

Willow in Blue Plate Chart—Bottom Left

Willow in Blue Plate Chart—Bottom Middle

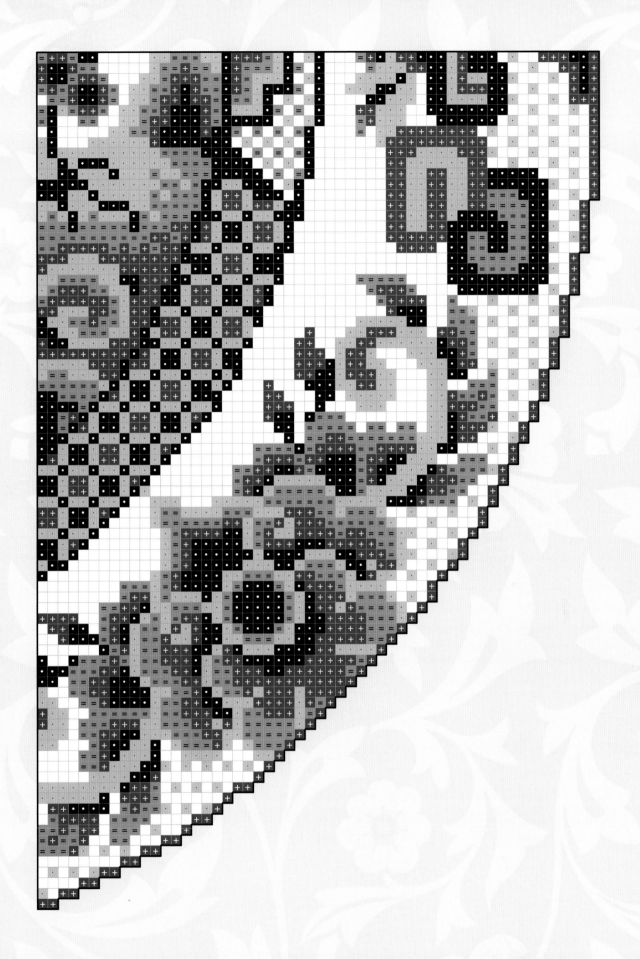

Willow in Blue Plate Chart—Bottom Right

Wreath Ornament

This design should be stitched on #16 duo canvas, using Delica beads.

Stitch count: 41 x 41

Materials required:
Beads:
  #2 bugle beads:

  green iris (20)
  matte red AB (80)
Delica beads:
  gold iris (160)
  matte galvanized silver (949)
  matte light green AB (386)
  matte medium green iris (425)
  matte metallic dark green (224)

6/0 seed beads, matte red AB (19)
11/0 seed beads, matte red (79)

Misc:
#16 duo canvas, 5" square
Fabric for backing, 4" square
Lightweight cardboard
Needles
Scissors
Washable jewelry glue

Instructions:
1. Refer to Photo 1. Stitch as charted below, leaving white areas unbeaded.

Bead Code

  gold iris

  matte medium green iris

  matte metallic dark green

matte galvanized silver

 matte light green AB

Wreath Ornament Chart

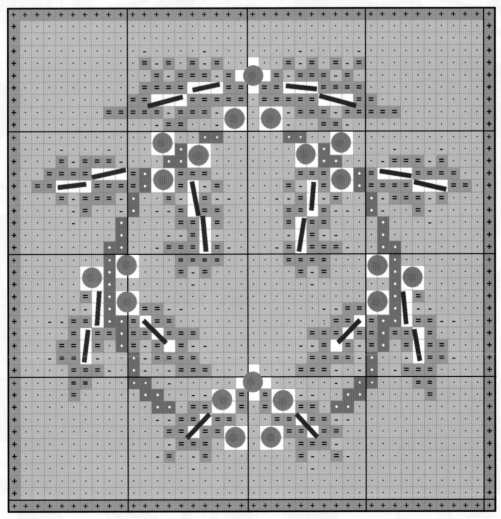

2. Refer to Photo 2. Sew on bugle beads in leaves as indicated on chart.

3. For berries, sew on matte red 6/0 beads, anchored with one 11/0 matte red seed bead.

4. Refer to Photos 3 and 4 and Diagram A. Sew on green Delica beads to create border, taking care to make corners as shown. Note: To avoid distortion, take care not to pull the thread too tightly when working the border.

Finishing:
1. Trim excess canvas to ⅜". Notch corners.

2. Use trimmed canvas as a template for backing. Cut backing fabric to same size. Notch corners.

3. Cut cardboard to ⅛" smaller all around than beadwork. Glue back side of beadwork onto cardboard, folding excess canvas onto back of cardboard and gluing it in place.

4. Press notched excess of backing to same size as beadwork. Slip-stitch backing and beadwork together so backing does not show from beaded side.

5. Sew matte red AB bugle beads all around edge of piece, where fabric meets beadwork. Sew each bead on individually, then run one connecting thread through all bugles to smooth the line. Bury excess thread in the backing fabric.

6. Add beaded handle, using a doubled strand of thread for strength. Bring needle out at top left of piece. Slip matte red 11/0 seed beads on needle and thread until there are 60 on the strand. Insert needle into top right of piece. Bury thread in backing.

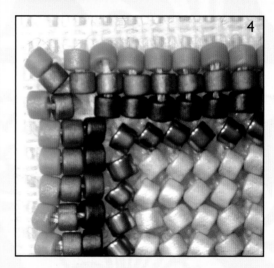

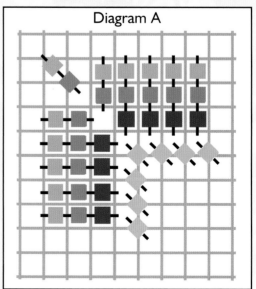

Diagram A

Yesteryear's Retreat

This design is stitched on #18 interlock canvas, using 15/0 seed beads. The finished size is 4" x 6" and fits nicely into a standard frame.

Stitch count: 72 x 108

Materials required:

Beads:

15/0 seed beads:

Ceylon light periwinkle (359)
Ceylon medium aqua (390)
lined light aqua (703)
lined medium green (609)
lined medium orchid (739)
lined pale pink (675)
lined topaz (485)
opaque dark brown (591)
opaque light amethyst (331)
opaque lustered red AB (198)
opaque lustered white (1238)
opaque matte black (641)
opaque rust (887)
opaque yellow (46)

Misc:

#18 interlock canvas, 7" x 9"
Needles
Scissors

Instructions:

1. Stitch as charted on pages 118–119.

Finishing:

1. Frame or finish as desired.

Bead Code

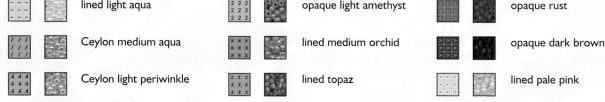

	lined light aqua		opaque light amethyst		opaque rust
	Ceylon medium aqua		lined medium orchid		opaque dark brown
	Ceylon light periwinkle		lined topaz		lined pale pink

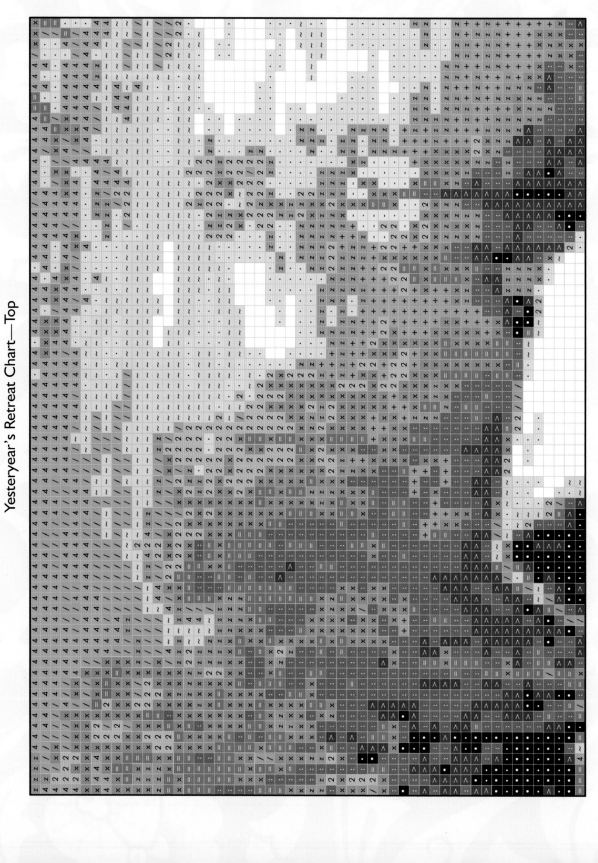

Bead Code

opaque lustered red AB		opaque yellow
lined medium green		opaque lustered white
opaque matte black		

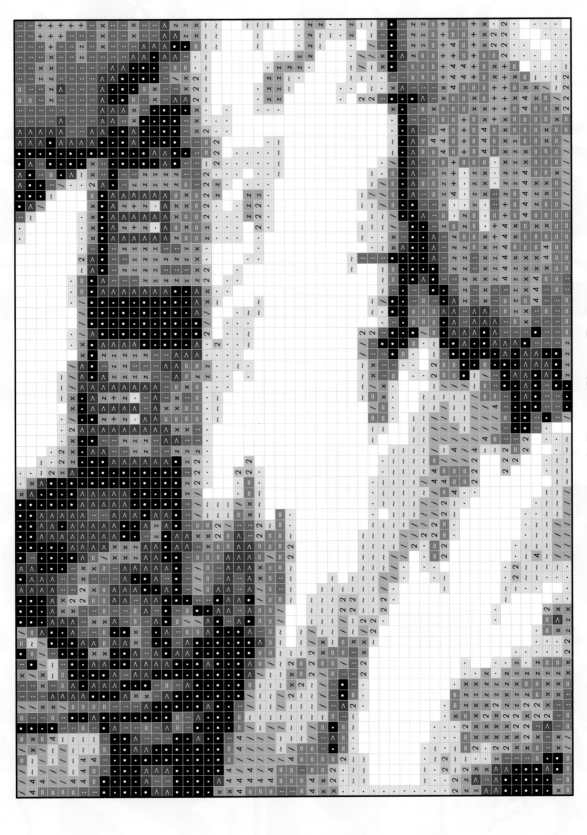

Yesteryear's Retreat Chart—Bottom

Design-It-Yourself Charts

The following blank charts are supplied to encourage you to design your own pieces within these specific canvas sizes and shapes.

Refer to the Beadpoint general information section on pages 8–25 for instruction on bead colors and matching canvas to bead sizes.

Blank Flap Purse Chart—Back (with flap)

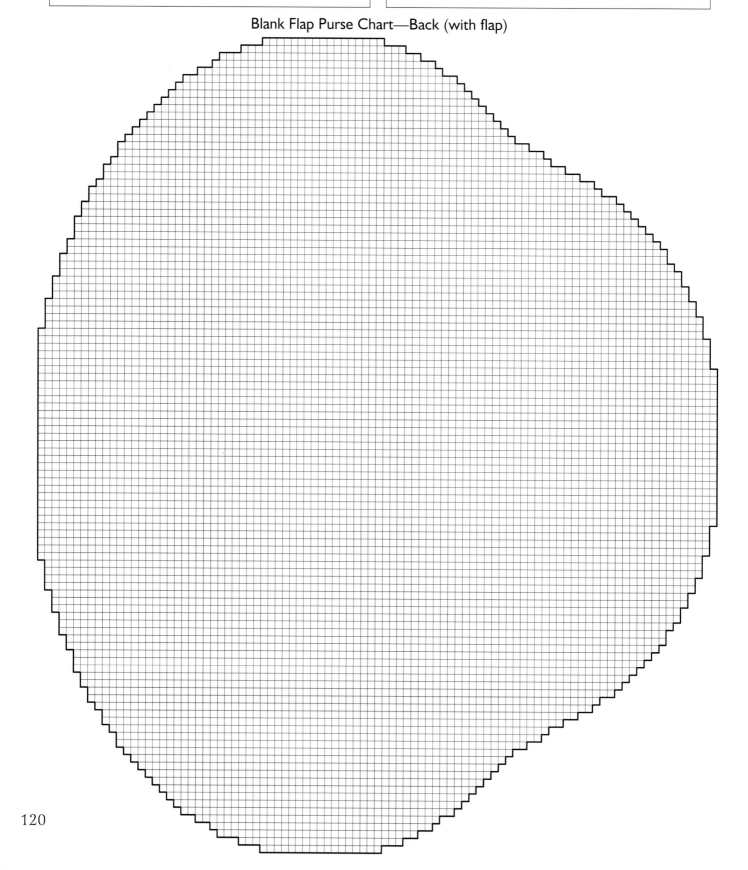

Blank Flap Purse Chart—Front

Blank Button Cover Chart

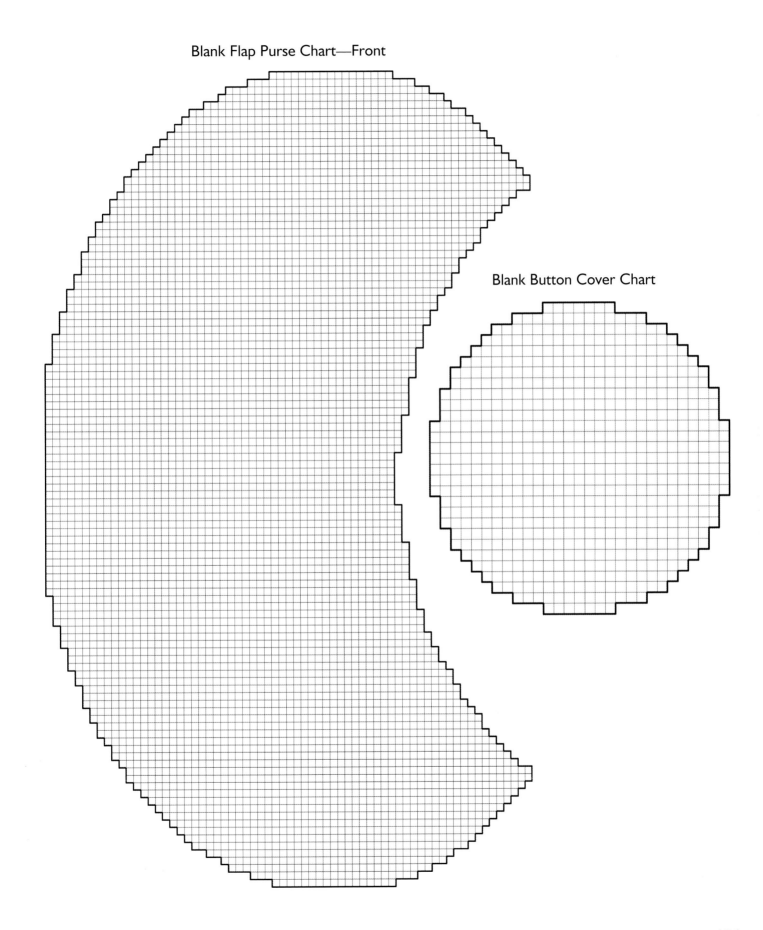

Blank Handled Purse Chart (for use with metal purse handle)

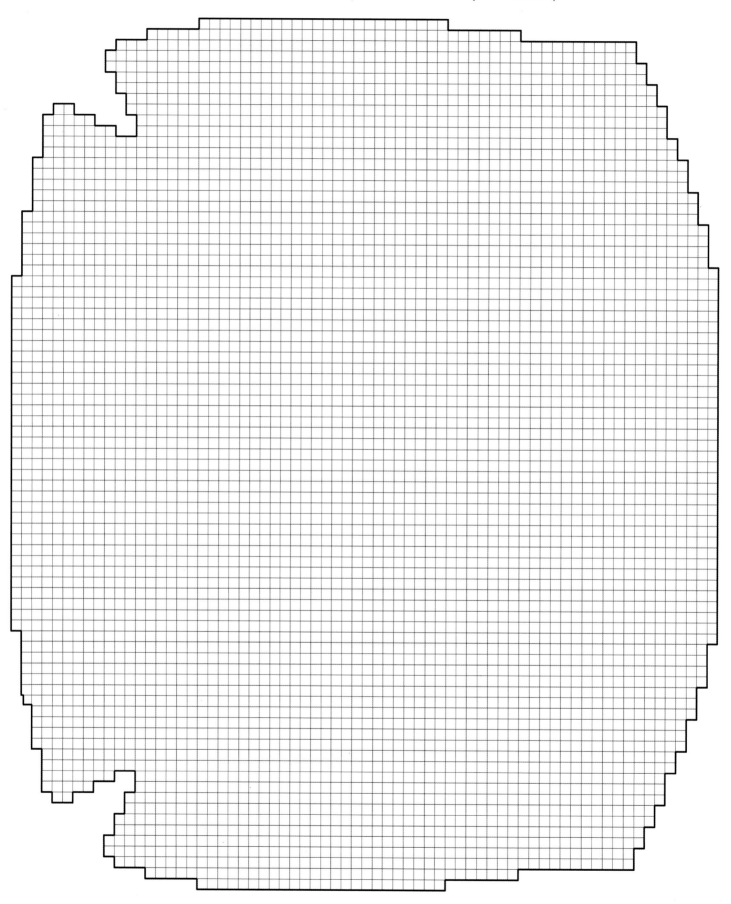

Blank Rectangle Canvas Chart—#14 Canvas

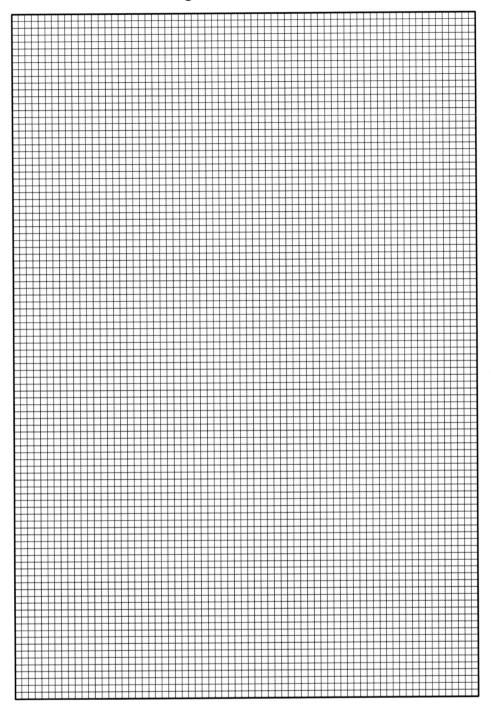

Blank Rectangle Canvas Chart—#16 Canvas

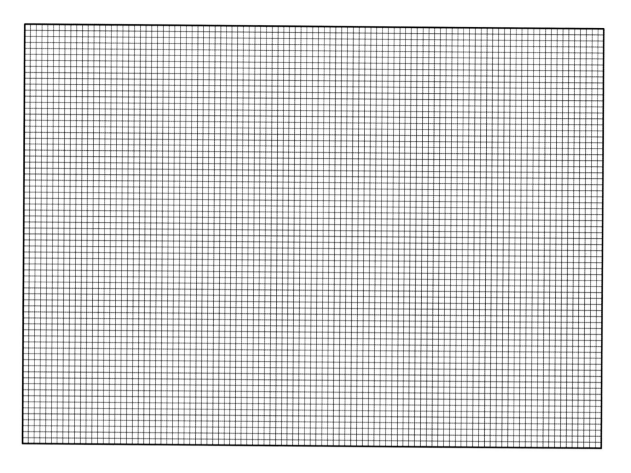

Blank Rectangle Canvas Chart—#18 Canvas

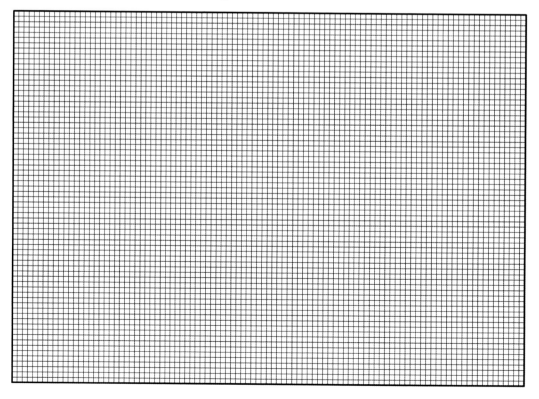

Blank Scissors Case Chart

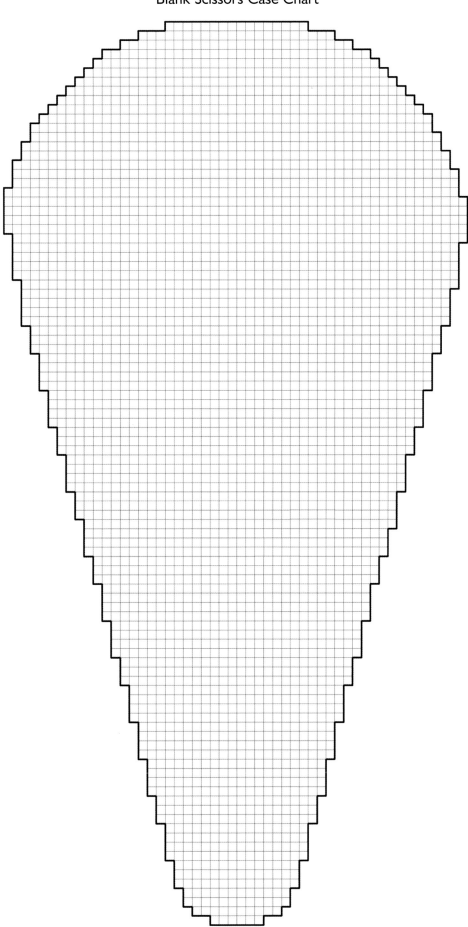

About the Author

Ann Benson has enjoyed a long and successful career as a designer of beadwork and various needle arts.

She is the author of *Beadweaving*, *Beadwear*, *Beadwork Basics*, *Two-Hour® Beaded Projects*, and *Beading for the First Time®* published by Sterling Publishing Co., Inc. She has also written three novels.

Ann lives in central Connecticut with her husband. She is the mother of two grown daughters.

photo courtesy of Bertelsman Publishing

Dedication

For my wonderful husband, Gary Frost.

Metric Equivalency Charts

mm-millimetres   cm-centimetres
inches to millimetres and centimetres

inches	mm	cm	inches	cm	inches	cm
⅛	3	0.3	9	22.9	30	76.2
¼	6	0.6	10	25.4	31	78.7
⅜	10	1.0	11	27.9	32	81.3
½	13	1.3	12	30.5	33	83.8
⅝	16	1.6	13	33.0	34	86.4
¾	19	1.9	14	35.6	35	88.9
⅞	22	2.2	15	38.1	36	91.4
1	25	2.5	16	40.6	37	94.0
1¼	32	3.2	17	43.2	38	96.5
1½	38	3.8	18	45.7	39	99.1
1¾	44	4.4	19	48.3	40	101.6
2	51	5.1	20	50.8	41	104.1
2½	64	6.4	21	53.3	42	106.7
3	76	7.6	22	55.9	43	109.2
3½	89	8.9	23	58.4	44	111.8
4	102	10.2	24	61.0	45	114.3
4½	114	11.4	25	63.5	46	116.8
5	127	12.7	26	66.0	47	119.4
6	152	15.2	27	68.6	48	121.9
7	178	17.8	28	71.1	49	124.5
8	203	20.3	29	73.7	50	127.0

yards to metres

yards	metres	yards	metres	yards	metres	yards	metres	yards	metres
⅛	0.11	2⅛	1.94	4⅛	3.77	6⅛	5.60	8⅛	7.43
¼	0.23	2¼	2.06	4¼	3.89	6¼	5.72	8¼	7.54
⅜	0.34	2⅜	2.17	4⅜	4.00	6⅜	5.83	8⅜	7.66
½	0.46	2½	2.29	4½	4.11	6½	5.94	8½	7.77
⅝	0.57	2⅝	2.40	4⅝	4.23	6⅝	6.06	8⅝	7.89
¾	0.69	2¾	2.51	4¾	4.34	6¾	6.17	8¾	8.00
⅞	0.80	2⅞	2.63	4⅞	4.46	6⅞	6.29	8⅞	8.12
1	0.91	3	2.74	5	4.57	7	6.40	9	8.23
1⅛	1.03	3⅛	2.86	5⅛	4.69	7⅛	6.52	9⅛	8.34
1¼	1.14	3¼	2.97	5¼	4.80	7¼	6.63	9¼	8.46
1⅜	1.26	3⅜	3.09	5⅜	4.91	7⅜	6.74	9⅜	8.57
1½	1.37	3½	3.20	5½	5.03	7½	6.86	9½	8.69
1⅝	1.49	3⅝	3.31	5⅝	5.14	7⅝	6.97	9⅝	8.80
1¾	1.60	3¾	3.43	5¾	5.26	7¾	7.09	9¾	8.92
1⅞	1.71	3⅞	3.54	5⅞	5.37	7⅞	7.20	9⅞	9.03
2	1.83	4	3.66	6	5.49	8	7.32	10	9.14

Index